Elementary Education in India: A Socio-Cultural Perspective

(D.El.Ed.-501)

For Diploma in Elementary Education [D.El.Ed.]

IMPORTANT STUDY MATERIAL FOR NIOS, SCERT, B.El.Ed. (DU), DIET, JBT, IGNOU

GULLYBABA PUBLISHING HOUSE PVT. LTD.

ISO 9001 & ISO 14001 CERTIFIED CO.

Developed and Produced by:
GullyBaba Publishing House (P) Ltd.

Regd. Office:
2525/193, 1st Floor, Onkar Nagar-A,
Tri Nagar, Delhi-110035
(From Kanhaiya Nagar Metro Station
Towards Old Bus Stand)
Ph. 011-27387998, 27384836, 27385249

Branch Office:
1A/2A, 20, Hari Sadan,
Ansari Road, Daryaganj,
New Delhi-110002
Ph. 011-23289034
011-45794768

E-mail: hello@gullybaba.com, Website: GullyBaba.com
First Edition: 2017

Price: ₹220/-

Author: Gullybaba.Com Panel
ISBN: 978-93-86276-46-9

Preface

The Indian State is well aware of the importance of ensuring universal basic education. There have been important Constitutional amendments as well that were intended to give a boost to elementary education. The 42nd Amendment to the Constitution in 1976 brought education, which was largely a state responsibility, into the Concurrent List and made universalizing elementary education the responsibility of both the central and state governments. Many positive developments have been recorded, especially after the 1990s. Demand for basic education continues to grow with increasing recognition of the importance of educating children among parents and guardians.

The present GPH book ***"Elementary Education in India: A Socio-Cultural Perspective (Course-501)"*** presents an overview of the elementary education at the national and global levels. The main aim of book is to describe the historical progression of elementary education to help the teachers understand the nature and development of elementary education in a holistic way. This book will be very helpful in fair understanding of elementary education in the contemporary Indian society.

The book is written specially in question & answer format to provide students the instant gratification of a correct answer. In this book, we have tried to solve all possible questions from the exams' point of view. Solutions of previous years questions papers have also been included to help students to understand the unique examination structure.

We hope that this book would not only be a favourite study material for the students but also can be a nice resource for teaching.

An attempt has been carefully made to present this book more useful and meet the requirement and challenges of the course prescribed by Indian Universities/Colleges.

We wish you a successful and rewarding career ahead. Feedback in this regard is solicited.

– Gullybaba.Com Panel

Acknowledgement

Our compliments go to the **GullyBaba Publishing House (P) Ltd.,** and its meticulous team who have been enthusiastically working towards the perfection of the book.

Their teamwork, initiative and research have been very encouraging. Had it not been for their unflagging support, this work wouldn't have been possible. The creative freedom provided by them along with their aim of presenting the best to the reader has been a major source of inspiration in this work. Hope that this book would be successful.

– Gullybaba.Com Panel

Publisher's Note

The present book D.El.Ed.-501 is targeted for examination purpose as well as enrichment. With the advent of technology and the Internet, there has been no dearth of information available to all; however, finding the relevant and qualitative information, which is focused, is an uphill task.

We at **GullyBaba Publishing House (P) Ltd.,** have taken this step to provide quality material which can accentuate in-depth knowledge about the subject. GPH books are a pioneer in the effort of providing unique and quality material to its readers. With our books, you are sure to attain success by making use of this powerful study material. Provided book is just a reference book based on the syllabus of particular University/Board. For a profound information, see the textbooks recommended by the University/Board.

Our site **gullybaba.com** is a vital resource for your examination. The publisher wishes to acknowledge the significant contribution of the Team Members and our experts in bringing out this publication and highly thankful to Almighty God, without His blessings, this endeavor wouldn't have been successful.

– Publisher

Topics Covered

Contents

Question Papers

Elementary Education in India: A Retrospect

INTRODUCTION

Elementary education plays a very significant role in democratic system. Our constitutional framers realised the value of elementary education as long back as 1950's and made a provision for free and compulsory education for all children up to the age of 14. In fact, education up to this stage is regarded as general and basic education. Universalisation of Elementary Education (UEE) has become a global concern today. Universalisation of elementary education means making available elementary education to every child. Education was imparted in Gurukulas, which were mostly located slightly away from the habitations. From time to time, Government of India reviewed the position of Education, particularly elementary education (viz. in 1968, 1986 and in 1992-the latest is NCF 2005) and formulated policies regarding education. These policies had salutary effect on the process of propagating elementary education.

Q1. Briefly discuss Ancient Indian Education.

Or

Discuss the education system in ancient period.

Ans. In ancient India, every aspect of life including education was influenced by religion. However, it is worth to mention that education aimed at many-sided development of the personality of the student of course with a religious orientation. The concept, aims and ideals of education were correlated with the ideals of life. Religion played an imperative part in life in ancient India. The whole social structure of those days was religious and the whole system of education surged with religious atmosphere. Teachers were usually priests, so they provided Liberal, Spiritual and Religious education. In ancient India, the whole system of education ran on the specific system of institution called 'Gurukul System of Education'. The main sources of teaching in the ancient education were Vedic literature which represent the most important and intrinsic part of life of the Indian people.

In Vedic period, as the period is known, teacher or Guru used to give knowledge to their pupil on the basic of Vedic literature which consisted of eight different forms; they are Four Vedas, Six Vedangas, Four Upavedas, Four Brahmanas, One hundred and eight Upanishads, Six systems of Philosophy, Bhagavad Gita, and Three Smritis. The Vedas deal with every branch of knowledge and provide basic material of all arts and science. In fact, they are the first source of wisdom. Ancient educators considered knowledge as the third eye of man which gives him insight into all worldly and non-worldly matters. Teacher occupied a vital position in the Vedic system of education. The teacher was a parent surrogate, facilitator of learning, exemplar and inspirer, confident, detector friend and philosopher, evaluator, imparter of knowledge and wisdom and above all a guru, religious and spiritual guide. Therefore, spirituality, character building, personality development, civic sense, promoting efficiency, preservation and propagation of culture were the set goals and aims of education. In Vedic period, forest was treated as a centre of education, which was far from the madding crowd's ignoble strife. In ancient time people used to live a simple and a pious life. They used to perform their duties and responsibilities with utmost care and devotion. Everyone had certain moral values and they considered following religion norms as their duty. They used to live in closed contact with saints, which made their life religious.

Fig. 1.1: Ancient education system

Under ancient or more particularly Vedic education process, all human beings would make necessary or positive changes in their behaviours. It was with feelings of love and devotion that atmosphere of educational institution was charged with. An important objective of ancient educational system was to preserve and transmit ancient Indian culture. Renowned teachers, who used to engage in their work continuously, were performing this task. Habits of performing various functions independently were developed in student, which used to help them in uplifting their future life. The ancient education system had been able to develop the all-round behaviour of student. However, the system did not have a written curriculum yet, Gurus would choose those activities that helped to develop different dimensions of student's personality. To reiterate, the overall system of education in ancient India was based on Vedas. Vedas are considered to be main source of Indian philosophy of life. Among the four Vedas, the Rig Veda is considered as most fundamental from point of education as it is in this Veda that knowledge aspect is being interpreted and four stages of human life are also dealt in the Rig Veda. In the Gurukul system of education, the Brahmin Gurus or teachers taught children of only three upper casts of Aryan society, namely, Brahmins, Kshatriyas and Vaishyas. The education for non-Aryans was kept in dark, although they are in the majority among the Indian populace. The majority of the pupils were boys or male, but there was a provision for the girl's education also, but the number of schools or Gurukul which were exclusively for girls were very few in those days.

In ancient period, the Indian society was divided into four different Varnas also known as Chatur Varna on the basis of their work. That is why the Brahmins worked as the teachers and the priest of the temples. The subjects of the ancient education were basically Philosophy, grammar and logic. The system of education in those days was not only theoretical but a practical content that included meditation, seminars, and religious practices. With the combination of theoretical knowledge and the practical knowledge the pupil used to develop the healthy civic and aesthetic sense and it was impossible to lead a successful life without it. After getting education from Gurukuls, students were empowered to get married and lead a family life. After marriage the civil life used to begin, from there onwards it became their duty to obey all the norms and values set by the society. To perform various kinds of duties towards their family and for the society was their prime responsibility, for which they were being educated in Gurukuls.

Q2. Discuss the concept of 'guru'. Evaluate the role and responsibilities of guru in ancient Indian culture.

Or

Describe the role and responsibilities of Guru under the Gurukul system. [April-2016, Q.No.-41]

Ans. In the ancient Indian education system, the 'guru' (teacher) was the institutional answer for a socio-philosophical-historical context. Great importance was attached to the teachers in the ancient system of education. The guru was a person totally dedicated to the transmission of knowledge.

The education system of ancient period has unique characteristic and qualities which were not found in the ancient education system of any other country in the world. Gurukul (ashram) was a type of school in ancient India, residential in nature, with students living in proximity to the teacher (guru). Guru was the head of Gurukul, a father figure, parent and guardian of the inmates. In a gurukul, students would reside together as equals, irrespective of their social standing, learnt from the guru and distribute work in themselves to help the guru in his day-to-day life. At the end of studies, students would be ready to offer gurudakshina (one time fees) to the guru.

Guru was revered more than parents and enjoyed a unique status, even higher than that of gods:

गुरूर्ब्रह्मा गुरूर्विष्णुः, गुरूर्देवो महेश्वरः।

गुरूर्साक्षात परब्रह्मः, तस्मै श्री गुरूवे नमः।।

The Guru was an epitome of good qualities of head, heart and hand, spirituality, knowledge, scholarship. A true teacher was supposed to be student till the of his life. He was 'Guide by the side', not the 'Sage on the stage'.

Role and Responsibilities: In Bhartiya Darshan 'Guru' has significant place. It consists of two words, Gu-ru. The word 'Gu' indicated darkness and 'ru' means controller. It means to avoid darkness or ignorance. In Vedas the term achariya is used for guru. Guru is considered greatest treasure of knowledge.

Guru was playing many roles in those days for the students like parent, teacher, scholar, missionary, a friend-philosopher and a guide. He was to pay personal attention to the needs of the students. It was a responsibility of Guru to see that the student develops, makes progress to the satisfaction of Guru as well as to his own satisfaction. That time the relationship between teachers used to be very intimate and the taught-like father and son.

Oral interaction method was prevalent those days. Lectures, discourses, a debates and discussions, recitation and recapitulation were part of routine daily student life. Assessment was continuous comprehensive assessment internally conducted by Guru. There were no terminal examinations, no degree-certificates, but announcing by the Guru in the convocation that the student has graduated after completion of the stipulated studies. Guru would present the qualified student to a gathering of learned people who may ask questions, or the student would be asked to contest in debate and prove himself. Then for his mastery over the subject, the student would be known and accepted as a scholarly person.

Learners' autonomy was respected. They were free to choose the Guru and the subject of study. At the same time, to accept the student (Shishya) or not, it was a prerogative of the Guru, the teacher.

Q3. Explain the characteristics of today's teacher.

Ans. Some of the characteristics that a teacher today needs to acquire and develop are as follows:

- Listener - to students in an empathetic manner
- building trust and appreciation through personal interaction and involvement.
- Organised – systematic, working in a planned manner
- Knowledgeable - is in a constant quest for knowledge
- Compassionate - caring, empathetic and able to respond to people at a feeling level. Open with personal thoughts and feelings, encouraging others to do so.
- Creative - versatile, innovative, and open to new ideas
- Open and positive - think positively- encourage others also to be positive
- Communicative - share ideas with others encouraging effective communication
- Dependable – honest, open and authentic in working with others
- Patient – strives to be highly fair and objective
- Committed — to students and the profession
- Personable – establish and maintain positive mutual working relationships while
- Individually perceptive - sees each student as a unique and valuable individual
- Value based - focuses upon the worth and dignity of human beings.
- Sensitive to community values.
- Self-confident and poised, encourage students to develop a positive self-concept.
- Motivated - enthusiastic with standards and expectations
- Constructive - in thoughts actions.

Q4. What do you know about the Macaulay's Minute? Briefly discuss about 'Downward Filtration Theory'.

Or

What were the main aims of introducing English system of education in India according to the Macaulay's Minute?

Ans. Macaulay wrote his famous minute on Feb. 2, 1835 in which he vehemently criticized almost everything Indian: astronomy, culture, history, philosophy, religion etc., and praised everything western. On this basis he advocated the national system of education for India which could best serve the interest of the British Empire. His minutes was accepted and Lord William Bentinck issued his proclamation in march 1935 which set at rest all the controversies and led to the formulation of a policy which became the corner stone of all educational programmes during the British period in India.

Lord Macaulay, participating in the debate, the Chairman of the General Committee of Public Instruction, prepared and circulated a memorandum on the issue in January 1835. He took a decisive stand against the native culture and learning, native knowledge and languages like Sanskrit, Arabic and Persian and asserted on the education of Western Science through English language. His views have gone as (in) famous Macaulay's Minute (2) in the history of Indian education.

Main Aim of Introducing English system of Education in India

Macaulay wrote in his minute –we must at present do our best to form a class of persons Indian in blood and colour and English in taste, opinions in morals and in intellect. Macaulay's arguments in favour of English. He rejected the claims of Arabic and Sanskrit as against English, because he considered that English was better than either of them. His arguments in favour of English were:

(1) It is the key to modern knowledge and is therefore more useful than Arabic or Sanskrit.

(2) It stand pre eminent even among the language of the west in India, English is the language sponsored by the ruling class. It is likely to become the language of commerce throughout the seas of the east.

(3) It would bring about renaissance in India, just as Greek or Latin's did in England or just as the languages of western Europe in civilized Russia.

(4) The natives are desirous of being taught English and are not eager to learn Sanskrit or Arabic.

(5) It is possible to make the natives of this country good English scholar, and to that end our efforts ought to be directed.

(6) It was impossible to educate the body of people but it was possible through English education to bring about –a class of persons Indian in blood and colour and English in taste, opinions in morals and in intellect‖, and that education was to filter down from them to the masses.

Downward Filtration Theory: The British rulers thought that in order to run the administration peacefully and smoothly it was essential to make the higher classes' blind followers of the Britishers. This they wanted to achieve through educating classes. This theory meant–education is to be filtered to the common people. Drop by drop , the education would go to the common public so that at due time it may take the form of a vast stream which remained water desert of the society starved for water for a long time and high class of people would be educated and common people would gain influence from them.

Macaulay's Minute and policy of the 'Downward Filtration Theory' was accepted by Lord Bentinck, the Governor General, on behalf of the

British rule and he passed the orders to accept English language as a medium of instruction for the Indian education system.

Q5. Write the objectives and the main recommendations of Woods' Dispatch.

Ans. The Wood's Dispatch of 1854 is known as Magna Carta of Indian Education. It aimed at spread of English language and Western knowledge through English or Indian languages.

Aims and objectives of Wood's Dispatch

(1) To confer upon the natives of India those vast and material blessings which flow from the general diffusion of western knowledge.

(2) To raise the moral character.

(3) To provide the East India Company with educated, reliable and capable public servants.

(4) To secure for U. K a large and assumed supply of many articles necessary for her manufacturers.

(5) To make people of India familiar with the works of European authors.

Main Recommendations of Wood's Dispatch:

(1) Government's acceptance of educational responsibility: The Dispatch for the first time clearly accepted that the responsibility of education in India lies on British Government.

(2) Aims of education: The Dispatch defined the aim of education keeping in view the interests of Indians and British rule. Education is to raise intellectual fitness and moral character of Indians. At the same time, it was to prepare them to become supporters of British rule in India.

(3) Oriental languages: The Dispatch emphasized the importance of Oriental languages. Mr. Wood had recognized the usefulness of Sanskrit, Arabic and Persian and recommended them as subjects of study in regular institutions. Like Macaulay, he also recognized the usefulness of western knowledge for Indians.

(4) Medium of instruction: The Dispatch recommended that owing to the shortage of books in Indian languages, the medium of instruction should be English. But English should be needed for those people who have proper knowledge and taste for English and are able to understand European knowledge through this language. For other Indian languages should be used.

(5) Establishment of Education Department: The Dispatch directed that the Department of Public Instruction should be established in every province. This department was to inspect schools and to guide teachers.

(6) **Establishment of Universities:** The Dispatch recommended the establishment of Universities in Presidency towns of Calcutta, Bombay and Madras, and if necessary at other places also.

(7) **Establishment of graded schools:** The Dispatch recommended that there should be graded schools all over the country as follows:

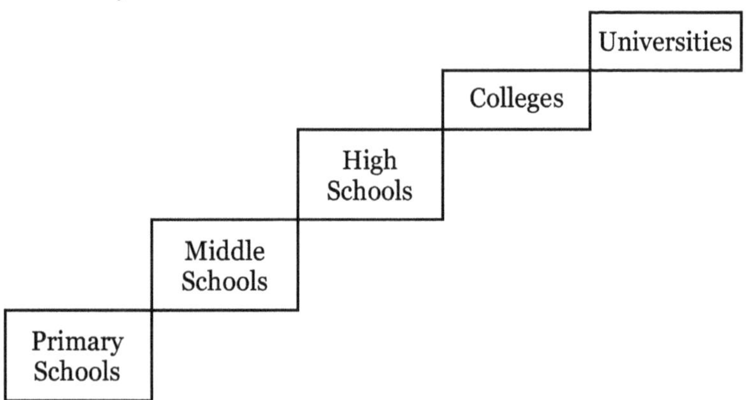

Fig. 1.2

(8) **Expansion of mass education:** The Dispatch admitted that mass education has been totally neglected. Therefore, the Dispatch directed that useful and practical knowledge should be conveyed to masses. To achieve this purpose, the Dispatch recommended the establishment of increased number of High Schools, Middle Schools and Primary Schools. The indigenous primary schools were regarded as the foundation upon which the superstructure of education could be constructed.

(9) **Grant-in-aid System:** The Dispatch proposed the sanction of grant-in-aid to the Indian educational institutions for increase in teacher's salaries, scholarships, libraries, construction of building etc.

Following types of educational institutions were declared eligible for grants:

(i) Institutions following the rules and regulations enforced by the government and which were prepared to get them inspected by government inspectors.

(ii) Institutions run very well by private institutions.

(iii) Institutions free from the communal feelings and not observing distinction of caste, community and creed.

(iv) Institutions charging fees from the students.

(10) **Training of Teachers:** Without proper training, teachers would not be able to teach well. The Dispatch recommended

the need for establishing different types of training institutions.

(11) **Education of women:** In Wood's Dispatch, much emphasis was given upon women education. The Dispatch recommended that the education ladder would be incomplete without women education. It appreciated the work of enlightened Indians engaged in this sacred job.

(12) **Muslim Education:** Concerning Muslim Education, Mr. Wood found that Muslims in this country were educationally backward and hence they should be encouraged to gain more education and efforts should be made in this direction.

(13) **Vocational Education:** The Dispatch pointed out the need of starting vocational schools and colleges for imparting instructions in different vocations. Vocational education may be considered as a necessity in order to prepare children for future life.

(14) **Education for Employment:** The Dispatch recommended that academically and highly qualified person should be preferred more than the others for Government services.

(15) **Policy of religious neutrality:** The Dispatch directed the company to follow a policy of religious neutrality. No man's religion was to stand in the way of securing an appointment under the Government. Moreover, no religious instruction should be imparted in educational institutions. They were to be exclusively secular.

Q6. Write short notes on the following:

(i) Hunter Commission

Ans. The Hunter Commission recommended that at the high school stage there ought to be two distinctive streams of education - one for preparing the students for higher education and the other for practical occupations. In other words, it emphasised the bifurcation of courses at the upper classes of the high school - one leading to the entrance examination (matriculation) of the universities and the other for practical life; preparing youth for commercial or non-literary pursuits. This recommendation was accepted and an alternative examination to the institution's examination was started to be organised in every province. But the scheme remained unpopular as not even one-tenth of the students who appeared for matriculation came forward for the other stream, i.e. for the alternative examination.

(ii) Universities Commission:

Ans. Lord Curzon was the first person to appoint a commission on university education. On January 27, 1902, the Indian Universities Act, 1904-Indian University Commission was appointed under the Chairmanship of Sir Thomas Raleigh to enquire into the conditions and prospects of the universities established in British India and to consider and report upon the proposals for improving their constitution and working. The Commission recommended the reorganisation of university administration; a much more strict and systematic supervision of the colleges by the university; and the imposition of more exacting conditions of affiliation.

The Indian Universities Act of 1904, passed on March 21, was formulated on the basis of the recommendations of the Indian University Commission 1902.

(iii) Sadler Commission

Ans. "No Satisfactory reorganisation or university system will be possible unless and until a radical reorganisation of the system of secondary education upon which university works depend is carried into effect."

This commission is also known as 'Calcutta University Commission." This commission was appointed in 1917 under the Chairmanship of Michael Sadler. Therefore, it is known as Sadler Commission. The main purpose of this Commission was to make improvements in the functioning of Calcutta University. But it also suggested some points regarding the drawbacks in Secondary Education. At the same time, it gave certain valuable suggestions for the Improvements in Secondary Education. The main recommendations of this commission were:

(1) There should be a provision for diversified courses at secondary stage of education.

(2) The minimum qualification for getting admission in Universities should be intermediate and not Matriculation.

(3) Intermediate colleges should be set up under universities. They should provide education in different fields like Science, Medicine, Engineering and Arts etc.

(4) Boards of Secondary and Intermediate Education should be established in every province. These Boards will look after the administration and control of Secondary Education.

(5) The medium of instruction in high schools should be mother tongue.

(iv) The Hartog Committee

Ans. Hartog Committee (1929) suggested diversification of curricula and diversion of students into industrial and commercial careers. The outcome of this recommendation was that provincial governments started technical, commercial or agricultural high schools and also began to give large grants to assist school which provided non-literary courses. This development helped in the introduction of some effective measures for providing alternative vocational or prevocational courses at the secondary stage.

(v) The Sapru Committee

Ans. This committee was established by UP (Uttar Pradesh) Government to study the problems related to unemployment. The committee found that the main cause of unemployment is faulty education system. It also made one thing clear that the present education system prepares the student only for the examination. It provides them degrees and certificates, not employment. The committee made certain recommendations to improve it–

(1) The intermediate stage should be abolished i.e. inter classes should be abolished. In the place of this duration of classes of Secondary Education should be increased by one more year. The duration of middle classes should be 6 years. It should be further divided into two stages–lower stage and higher stage.

(2) There should be a provision for diversified courses in middle classes.

(3) Vocational Education should be started after lower stage of middle classes.

(4) There should be three years degree course at University stage.

(vi) The Abbot-Wood Report

Ans. Although many commissions and committees were formed till now, they made their recommendations and a lot of work was done. But still there were many problems in the Education like educational organisation, problems of vocational education etc. The Government of India invited the experts. Mr. A. Abbot and Mr. S.H. Wood, to study the problems related to education and to give their suggestion for solving these problems. They submitted their report in 1937, which, was popularly known as 'Abbot-Wood Report.'

They studied the problems and recommended that separate vocational Institutes or polytechnics should be established in parallel with the hierarchy of schools of academic courses. On their recommendations various polytechnics, technical and agricultural schools were established. These will help in removing the problem of unemployment.

Q7. Discuss about the Wardha Scheme, 1937.

Ans. Wardha Scheme is also known as Nai Talim or Basic Education or Buniyadi Talim (Shiksha) or Basic Shiksha. The scheme is an outcome of the philosophy of Gandhiji. It was given a definite shape by the committee under the chairmanship of Dr Zakir Hussain who later on became the President of India. Gandhian philosophy of education is a dynamic concept. It provides for the fulfilment of men's needs at all levels–biological, social and psychological. He believed that education should bring development of the whole man. He emphasised free, compulsory, and universal education for age groups of 7 to 14 years; and also that education should be imparted in one's mother language.

Some of the main features of the scheme are as follows:

(i) Every individual should learn to earn his living through manual work in life. Hence, education through manual labour is insisted. It is also considered non-violent, since an individual does not snatch away the living of others.

(ii) Learning is closely coordinated with home, community and the child's life activities, as well as, village crafts and occupations.

(iii) The entire education is to be imparted through some industry or vocation with a basic craft as the center of instruction. The idea is not to teach some handicraft along with liberal education, but education integrated with a handicraft is to be imparted through samavaaya (Samavay) integration method. It's a work-centric education.

(iv) Education is to be self-supporting to the extent of covering teachers' salaries and aims at making pupils self-supporting after the completion of their course.

Q8. Write a note on Sargent Report.

Or

Why central advisory board prepared "The Sargent Report" under the unversalisation of elementary education?

Ans. The Central Advisory Board of Education prepared a plan of educational development in India and submitted it to the Executive Council of the Governor-General for consideration. Sargent Report or Report for the Post-War Educational Development in India (by John Sargent, himself an educational consultant) is said to be a continuation of the Abbott and Wood Report as regard to the educational policy of the Government in the British rule. However, it was the first attempt to plan a national system of education for India. The Objectives of the plan included, "to create, in a period of not less than forty years, the same standard of educational attainments as had already been admitted in England."

The Report starts with these words–"Upon the education of the people of this country the fate of this country depends." Among other things, it provided for:

(i) Universal, compulsory and free Primary or Basic education for all children between the ages of 6 and 14; divided into the Junior Basic (6-11) and Senior Basic (11-14);

(ii) High School education for six years for selected children between the ages of 11 and 17.

(iii) Technical, commercial and art education for full-time and part-time students on an adequate scale.

The Report says, "High school education should not be considered simply as a preliminary to University education but a stage complete in itself, the large majority of high school learners should receive an education that will fit them for direct entry into occupations or professions".

The Report recommended the organisation of two main types of schools-the Academic and the Technical. It says,

"The Academic High School will impart instruction in the arts and pure sciences, while the Technical High School will provide training in the applied sciences, and industrial and commercial subjects. In both types the course in the Junior departments covering the present Middle stage will be very much the same and there will be a common core of the 'humanities' throughout. Art and Music should form an integral part of the curriculum in both and all girls should take a course in domestic science. In smaller centres, which can only be served economically by single High Schools, the individual schools should be required to offer as wide a choice of courses as possible. In rural areas an agricultural bias should be given to the curriculum."

Sargent Report laid a good deal of stress on industrial and vocational education. It suggested for the full time and part time instructions in order to fulfil the requirement of the different categories of the skilled hands.

Q9. Elucidate the Radhakrishnan Commission, 1948-1949.

Ans. The University Education Commission, 1948-49, popularly known as the Radhakrishnan Commission, was appointed soon after independence under the chairmanship of Prof. S. Radhakrishnan. The Report is a document of great significance as it has guided the development of higher education in India and for its recommendations regarding university education. The recommendations which directly dealt with Centre-State relations in higher education administration included issues regarding the constitutional position of higher education, national policy, establishment of UGC, university autonomy, finance, etc.

On the Constitutional position of higher education, the Commission was in favour of including university education in concurrent list. The Commission pointed out that after independence, education, especially higher education assumed new dimensions and there was a need for development of responsibilities of universities in a wider perspective i.e., "the all India aspects of University education, the repercussions and interchanges necessary and desirable between universities and the need for a national guarantee of minimum standards of efficiency, make it impossible for university education to remain a purely Provincial (State) subject". Besides, the university had also to, provide leadership in politics and administration, in professions, industry and commerce. It had to meet the increasing demand for every type of higher education, literary and scientific, technical and professional.

Q10. Discuss in briefly about the Mudaliar Commission, 1952-53.

Or

Mudaliar Commission recommended which two types of institutions for teacher training?

[October-2016, Q.No.-31]

Ans. The Secondary Education Commission (1952-53), also known as Mudaliar Commission after the name of its Chairperson, recommended the re-organisation of the pattern of secondary education. As also recommended by the University Education Commission (now, Radhakrishnan Commission) (1948-49), it sought the addition of the intermediate stage, to increase the period of secondary education by one year and to plan a three-year degree course at the University stage in place of the prevalent two-year first degree course. It also recommended the diversification of curricula. The multipurpose schools contemplated were meant to provide terminal courses in Technology, Commerce, Agriculture, Fine Arts and Home Science and help to divert students to different walks of life and reduce pressure upon university entrance. It suggested agriculture as an important subject in rural schools as well as horticulture, animal husbandry and cottage industries. It recommended that girls in co-educational or mixed schools be taught subject like Home Science, Needle work, Drawing, Painting and Music.

The problems of teachers and teacher training programs was analysed by Mudaliar Commission, and recommended that there should be two types of institutions for teacher-training:

(i) **Primary Teacher Training Institutions** under the control of a separate board - to train those who have passed the School Leaving Certificate or Higher Secondary School Leaving Certificate for the period of two years; and

(ii) **Secondary Teacher Training Institutions** to be recognised by and affiliated to universities to train the graduates for the period of one academic year - planned to be extended to two academic years.

Teacher-trainees were expected to receive training in one or more of various extra-curricular activities. Training colleges were expected to, as a normal part of their work, arrange refresher courses, short intensive courses in special subjects, practical training through workshops and professional conferences.

Q11. Write a short note on the "National Committee on Women's Education, 1958".

Ans. The problems of education of girls and women in the country, acquired a new significance since the attainment of Independence. The Educational Panel of the Planning Commission, in July 1957, recommended that "a suitable Committee should be appointed to go into the various aspects of the question relating to the nature of education for girls at the elementary, secondary and adult stages and to examine whether the present system was helping them to lead a happier and more useful life". The Conference of the State Education Ministers in 1957 also agreed that a special committee should be appointed to examine the whole question of women's education.

In May 1958, the Government set up the National Committee on Women's Education, with Shrimati Durgabai Deshmukh as Chairman. The Committee, in its report published in 1959, recommended that the highest priority should be given to establishing a parity between the education of boys and girls and a bold and determined effort should be made by the Centre and the States to face the difficulties and magnitude of the problem. It recommended co-education upto the middle school stage but separate institutions for girls at the high school stage where more diversified curriculum suited to girls should be introduced. The Committee desired employment facilities for adult women, crèches, training of women teachers and ample provision for school mothers.

Q12. Why was the Kothari Commission appointed? Discuss its major recommendations.

Or

Explain the major goals of Kothari Commission. Also discuss some essential measures to implement CSS effectively.

Ans. The Education Commission which was appointed by the Govt. of India under the chairmanship of Dr. D.S. Kothari in 1964 and which gave its Report in 1966 is now popularly known as Kothari Commission. The Commission had to work on general principles and policies for development of education in all aspects and at all levels. The Commission observed education and research are crucial to the entire development and progress of a country-economic, cultural and spiritual. It condemned the rigidity that characteristed the existing system and emphasised the need for flexibility in educational policy to suit the changing circumstances. It hoped that the Report would provide some basic thinking and framework for taking the first step towards bringing educational revolution in India.

The Report made recommendations touching various sectors and aspects of education, the principal among those being:

(1) Introduction of work experience (which includes manual work, production experience, etc.) and social service as integral parts of general education at more or less all levels of education.

(2) Stress on moral education and inculcation of a sense of social responsibility. Schools should recognise their responsibility in facilitating the transition of youth from the world of school to the world of work and life.

(3) Vocationalisation of secondary education.

(4) The strengthening of centres of advanced study and the setting up of a small number of major universities which would aim to achieve highest international standards.

(5) Special emphasis on the training and quality of teachers for schools.

(6) Education for agriculture and research in agriculture and allied sciences should be given a high priority in the scheme of educational reconstruction.

(7) Development of quality and pace – setting institutions at all stages in all sectors.

(8) 10+2+3 was suggested as educational structure.

(9) 10 years general stream; vocationalisation of curriculum at +2 stage + college education of 3 years.

Goals stated by the commission:

(1) Education for inculcation of national values:

(a) Providing syllabus giving information about religions of the world.

(b) Presenting before students high ideas of social justice and social service.

(c) Encouraging students to meet in groups for silent meditation.

(d) Introducing moral, social and spiritual values.

(2) Educating for promoting social and national integration:

(a) Encouraging and enabling students to participate in community living.

(b) Developing all modern Indian language.

(c) Taking steps to enrich Hindi as quickly as possible.

(d) Introducing common school system of public education.

(3) Education for increasing productivity:

(a) Improving scientific and technological research and education at university level.

(b) Introducing S.U.P.W. as an integral part of general education.

(c) Make science a basic component of education and culture.

(d) Vocational education to meet the needs of the industry of agriculture.

(4) Education for an accelerating process of modernisation:

(a) Proper development of instruct attitudes and values and building essential skills like independent study.

(b) Adopting new methods of teaching

(c) Establishing universities of excellence in the country.

(d) Emphasising teaching of vocational subjects and science.

(e) Educating people of all straits of society.

Kothari Commission suggested some essential measures to implement common school system (CSS) effectively these are as follow:

(i) for elementary education increased national outlay to build required infrastructure to provide quality education, thereby transforming government, local and aided schools into genuine neighborhood schools,

(ii) at the primary level, free instruction for all in the mother tongue, in regional languages at the secondary level, and discontinuance of state aid to schools imparting education other than in the medium of mother tongue/ regional language,

(iii) phased implementation of the common school system within a ten year time frame, and essential minimum legislation, particularly to dispense with early selection processes, tuition fees, capitation fees etc. quality teacher education through:

- effective methods of teaching and evaluation
- revising the teacher education suitable for all stages of education.
- content course for clarification of basic concepts
- integrated course of general/professional education
- refreshing professional studies and conducting research, and
- practice teaching as a part of internship programme

Q13. What do you know about Yashpal Committee, 1992?

Ans. A National Advisory Committee was set up on 1 March 1992 by the Ministry of Human Resource Development under the Chairmanship of Prof. Yash Pal, former Chairman of the University Grants Commission (UGC), to advise on the ways and means to reduce the academic burden on school students. This committee is also known as Yashpal Committee. The Committee submitted its Report to the Ministry on 15 July 1993.

On receipt of the Report of the National Advisory Committee, a decision was taken by the Ministry to set up a Group under the Chairmanship of Shri Y. N. Chaturvedi, Additional Secretary, Department of Education of the Ministry, to examine the recommendations of the Committee, give its views on the feasibility of implementing them and a time schedule of implementation. The Group was set up on 25 August 1993 and a copy of the Government Order giving the composition.

Rewarding individual achievement, the committee discouraged the competitions – since they deprive children of joyful learning – and encouraged collaboration, group activities and group achievements to give a boost to cooperative learning in schools. For admission to early childhood education institutions, the Committee did not want any tests and interviews.

According to the Committee, the young children should not be compelled to carry very heavy bags of books everyday to schools. Textbooks should be treated as school property and thus, there should be no need for children to purchase the books individually and carry them daily to homes. The committee was of the opinion that in the primary classes, children should not be burdened with homework excepting for extension of explorations in the home environment. Homework, in the upper primary and secondary classes, where necessary, should be non-textual, and textbooks, when needed for work at home, should be made available on a rotation basis.

The committee suggested the concept based curriculum and textbooks for all subjects in primary classes. The committee has made observations regarding the syllabi and textbooks for all the subjects in primary classes. The committee observed that Language textbooks should adequately reflect the spoken idiom and give adequate representation to children's life experiences, imaginary stories and poems, and stories reflecting the lives of ordinary people in different parts of the country.

For granting recognition to private schools for improving the quality of learning, the Yashpal Committee wanted stringent norms. The committee appreciated the idea of setting up education committees at village, block and district level to undertake planning and supervision of schools under their jurisdiction.

For Primary Education, Yashpal Committee suggested the following quality criteria, they are:

(1) Percentage of attendance,

(2) Participation of the society,

(3) Rank attained in school grading,

(4) Quality standard of education could be determined on the basis of the criteria which include:

Work experience and Physical Education, Activities to give students various experiences and opportunities, Achievement of students in school tests, Class Management, Proceeding of Teaching, Arts, Usage of Educational material, Preparation of Teachers, Method of teaching, Study of environment, Surrounding, Action and participation of the students etc.

A rigorous, thorough and intensive teacher preparation programme was desired by the Yashpal Committee, resulting in satisfactory quality of learning in schools and enabling the trainee teachers to acquire the ability for self learning and independent thinking.

Q14. Discuss National Policy of Education (NPE), 1968. Explain the basic tenets of the policy.

Or

What is meant by 'equalisation of educational opportunity'? [October-2016, Q.No.-17]

Ans. In 1968, following the Report of the Education Commission (Kothari Commission) 1964-66, the Government of India issued a resolution on education policy, later known as the National Policy on

Education, 1968. The policy called for fulfilling compulsory education for all children up to the age of 14 and the better training and qualification of teachers, as stipulated by the Constitution of India.

The Government of India accordingly resolves to promote the development of education in the country in accordance with the following principles:

(1) **Free and Compulsory Education:** Strenuous efforts should be made for the early fulfillment of the Directive Principle under Article 45 of the constitution seeking to provide free and compulsory education for all children up to the age of 14. Suitable programmes should be developed to reduce the prevailing wastage and stagnation in schools and to ensure that every child who is enrolled in school successfully completes the prescribed course.

(2) **Status, Emoluments and Education of Teachers:** Of all the factors which determine the quality of education and its contribution to national development, the teacher is undoubtedly the most important.

(3) **Development of languages:** The energetic development of Indian Languages and literature is a sine qua non for educational and cultural development.

(4) **Equalisation of Educational Opportunities:** Strenuous efforts should be made to equalise educational opportunity. To promote social cohesion and national integration in the common school system as recommended by the Education Commission should be adopted.

(5) **Spread of Literacy and Adult Education:** The liquidation of mass illiteracy is necessary not only for promoting participation in the working of democratic institutions and for accelerating programmes of production, especially in agriculture, but for quickening the tempo of national development in general. Employees in large commercial, industrial and other concerns should be made functionally literate as early as possible.

(6) **Production of Books:** The quality of books should be improved by attracting the best writing talent. Immediate steps should be taken for the production of high quality text books for schools and universities.

(7) **Games and Sports:** Games and sports should be developed on a large scale with the objective of improving the physical fitness and sportsmanship of the average student as well as of those who excel in this department.

(8) **Part-time Education and Correspondence Courses:** Part-time education and correspondence courses should be developed on a large scale at the university stage. Such

facilities should also be developed for secondary school students, for teachers and for agricultural, industrial and other workers. Education through part - time and correspondence courses should be given the same status as full - time education. Such facilities will provide opportunities to the large number of people who have the desire to educate themselves.

Q15. Discuss about National Policy of Education (NPE), 1986 and its features.

Ans. The National Policy of 1986 was a remarkable step in the history of education in post-independence India. It aimed to promote national progress, a sense of common citizenship and culture; and to strengthen national integration.

Since the adoption of the National Policy, 1986, there has been considerable expansion in educational facilities all over the country at all levels. More than 90% of the rural habitation have been provided with primary schooling facilities within a radius of 1 km. Perhaps the most important development has been the acceptance of 10+2+3 as the national pattern of education throughout the country. In the school curricula in addition to common scheme of studies for boys and girls, science and mathematics were incorporated as compulsory subjects and work-experience assigned a place of importance.

Salient features of National Policy that emerged are:

(1) Operation Blackboard for UEE
(2) National system of education 10+2+3 system
(3) Accountability in education
(4) Women education
(5) Education for tribes/sc/st classes
(6) Equality
(7) Navodaya vidayalaa
(8) Common Educational structure
(9) National Curricular Framework with a Common Core
(10) Equality of Opportunity of Education
(11) Promote adult education.
(12) Vocationalisation

Q16. What were the major concerns of elementary education in India gleaned out from the recommendations of the commissions and the national policies?

Ans. Following were the major concerns of elementary education:

- Children living in rural areas continue to be deprived of a quality education because of their under qualified, untrained teachers. In recent years, to improve the professional training of rural teachers the number of qualified teachers has increased because of efforts by the government and private groups.
- Poor quality of instruction resulting in unsatisfactory quality of 'successful' students. Lack of instructional facilities and practices that build a stronger school program

- Substituting current examination system by alternatives like CCE
- In primary schools overall enrollment was found very low. Due to distance and lack of physical facilities etc., most of the 'out of the school children' don't go to school.
- Building positive mindset of teachers towards ICT
- High dropout rate-For variety of reasons the children leave school mostly, to work and earn money. A large percent of the dropouts are girls, because their parents forced them to leave school and tend the family at home.
- Inequality-Gender disparity, Urban-Rural disparity, regional disparity
- In pre-primary and elementary schools, strengthening of leadership and supervision by professional training and re-training of large number of personnel e.g. Teachers, Head Masters and Supervisors, etc.
- For rural schools obtaining more teachers is difficult because of state guidelines that approve of high student-teacher ratios.

Q17. Examine the structure of elementary education of 8 years.

Ans. In all parts of the country, it was thought advantageous to have a broadly uniform educational structure. The ultimate objective is to adopt the 10+2+3 pattern, the higher secondary stage of two years being located in schools, colleges or both according to local conditions.

National System of Education envisages a common educational structure in the pattern of 10+2+3 as suggested by Kothari Commission. This uniform structure of school education has been adopted all over the country. However, within the states, there remained variations in the number of classes constituting the Primary, Upper Primary, High and Higher Secondary school stages, age for admission to class I, medium of instruction, public examinations, teaching of Hindi and English, number of working days in a year, academic session, vacation periods, fee structure, compulsory education etc. The primary and upper primary or middle stages together constitute the elementary stage. The further break-up of the first 10 years was, elementary system comprising 5 years of primary education and 3 years of upper primary, followed by 2 years of High School.

Table 1.1: Structure of school education system in India

Stages of Schooling	Pre-Primary	Lower Primary	Upper Primary	Secondary	Higher Secondary
Grades	Nursery, LKG/KG	1 to 5	6 to 8	9 and 10	11 and 12
Length of program	3 years	5 years	3 years	2 years	2 years
Age level	Entry at 3 to 6 years	6 to 11 years	11 to 14 years	14 to 16 years	16 to 18 years

Pre-Primary: Pre-primary education forms the basis of learning in the broad structure of Indian education. It is divided into Nursery, Lower Kindergarten (LKG) and Upper Kindergarten (UKG). At this stage student is experienced with formal school life and reading and writing skills. It consists of children of 3-5 years of age.

Lower Primary: After finishing upper kindergarten or directly a child enters class one of primary school. In the lower primary level, students get an idea of the different subjects. The primary school curriculum emphasises general education and covers basic subjects such as reading, writing and arithmetic, supplemented by History, Civics and Geography as well as Environmental Science. At this stage, the children of the age group of 6-11 years study in the classes I-V in most of the states. However, in some of the states this stage consists of classes of I-IV. At the lower primary level, the language of instruction is generally the mother tongue, either Hindi or a regional language.

Upper Primary: Classes from sixth to eighth are called upper primary. From upper primary, other languages such as English and/or Hindi (if Hindi is not the mother tongue) are introduced.

Q18. Write a short note on National Curriculum Framework of 2005.

Or

Who proposed national framework for curriculum and for what purpose? [April-2016, Q.No.-16]

Or

What was the vision of the National Curriculum Framework, 2005? [October-2016, Q.No.-16]

Ans. The National Curriculum Framework (NCF 2005) is one of three National Curriculum Frameworks published in 1986, 2000 and 2005 by the National Council of Educational Research and Training NCERT in India. NPE 1986,92 proposed a national framework for curriculum as a means of evolving a national system of education. The document provides the framework for making syllabii, textbooks and teaching practices within the school education programmes in India. The NCF 2005 document draws its policy basis from earlier government reports on education as Learning Without Burden and National Policy of Education 1986-1992 and focus group discussion.

National Curriculum Framework was envisioned as a means of modernizing the system of education. National Curriculum Framework 2005 reviews and refers to the recommendations of the Mudaliar Commission and Kothari Commission and reviews development of Curriculum Framework of 1975, 1988 and 2000.

The NCF, 2005 examines the curriculum load on children in depth and provides a framework within which teachers are free to choose and provide the learning experiences that they think are useful for better learning. It envisages that in order to realise educational objectives, the curriculum functions as a structure that helps in providing required experiences.

Q19. What are the salient features of the revised NCF, 2005?

Or

The NCF, 2005 is based on which of our guiding principles? [April-2016, Q.No.-32]

Ans. Following are some of the salient features of the revised NCF, 2005:

(1) Guiding Principles: The fact that learning has become a source of burden and stress on children is an evidence of a deep distortion in educational aims and quality. To correct this distortion, the present National Curriculum Framework proposes five guiding principles for curriculum development:

- connecting knowledge to life outside the school,
- ensuring that learning is shifted away from rote methods,
- enriching the curriculum to provide for overall development of children rather than remain textbook centric,
- making examinations more flexible and integrated into classroom life and,
- nurturing an over-riding identity informed by caring concerns within the democratic polity of the country.

The National Curriculum Framework, while placing the learner as the constructor of knowledge, emphasises that curriculum, syllabus and textbooks should enable the teacher to organise classroom experiences in consonance with the child's nature and environment, and providing opportunities for all children. Significant changes are recommended in all the curricular areas with a view to making education more relevant to the present day and future needs in order to alleviate the stress children are coping with today. The NCF recommends the softening of subject boundaries so that children can get a taste of integrated knowledge and joy of understanding.

Language skills such as speech and listening, reading and writing – cut across school subjects and disciplines. Their foundational role in children's construction of knowledge right from elementary classes through higher secondary classes needs to be recognised. A renewed effort should be made to implement the three-language formula, emphasising the recognition of children's home language(s) or mother tongue(s) as the best medium of instruction. This includes tribal languages. English needs to find place along with other Indian languages. The multilingual character of Indian society should be seen as a resource for the enhancement of school life.

Teaching of Mathematics, it is proposed, should enhance the learner's resources to think and reason, visualise and handle abstractions, to formulate and solve problems.

Content, process and language of science teaching must be commensurate with the learner's age-range and cognitive reach. Science teaching should engage the learners in acquiring methods and processes that will nurture their curiosity and creativity, particularly in relation to the environment. Concern for the environment should be emphasised in every subject and through a wide range of activities involving outdoor project work.

Social Science learning in the NCF proposes to recognise the disciplinary markers while emphasising integration in Social Sciences from the perspective of marginalised groups. Gender justice and sensitivity towards tribal and dalit issues and minority sensitivities must inform all areas of Social Sciences.

Specifically to address the problem of curriculum load on children the review of the National Curriculum Framework, 2000 was initiated. Yashpal Committee had analysed this problem, tracing its roots to the system's tendency to treat information as knowledge. In its report, "Learning without Burden", the committee pointed out that learning at school cannot become a joyful experience unless we change our perception of the child as a receiver of knowledge and move beyond the convention of using textbooks as the basis for examination. The impulse to teach everything, to construct knowledge out of their experience arises from lack of faith in children's own creative instinct and their capacity.

"Learning without Burden" refers to a major change in the design of syllabi and textbooks. To make teaching a means of harnessing the child's creative nature, the report recommended a fundamental change in the system of examination, and also in the matter of organising the school curriculum.

(2) Critical Pedagogy: Teacher and student engagement is critical in the classroom because it has the power to define whose knowledge will become a part of school-related knowledge and whose voices will shape it. Students are not just young people for whom adults should devise solutions. They are critical observers of their own conditions and needs, and should be participants in discussions and problem solving related to their education and future opportunities. Hence, children need to be aware that their experiences and perceptions are important and should be encouraged to develop the mental skills needed to think and reason independently and have the courage to dissent. What children learn out of school — their capacities, learning abilities, and knowledge base — and bring to school is important to further enhance the learning process. This is all the more critical for children from underprivileged backgrounds, especially girls, as the worlds they inhabit and their realities are under-represented in school knowledge.

Participatory learning and teaching, emotion and experience need to have a definite and valued place in the classroom. While class participation is a powerful strategy, it loses its pedagogic edge when it is ritualised, or merely becomes an instrument to enable teachers to meet their own ends. From the experiences of both students and teachers true participation is started.

Q20. Discuss the implementations of NCF, 2005 for elementary school curriculum.

Ans. The immediate action is taken up at all the levels all over the country because of the resent of these developments on the educational scenario and the latest decision of implementing the RTE Act in all the states. The new curriculum is designed and implemented in most of the states following the NCF guidelines and NCERT has developed the new textbooks for all the subjects based on these reforms and philosophy and practice of education. Examinations are abolished and CCE is introduced at the elementary stage, participatory management is inducted making beneficiaries and community at large, partners to school complex in educating the young generations. In teaching-learning process, due emphasis on ICT involvement is also being given.

For the curriculum transaction, the total number of days is decided to be 200 days. The school annual calendar could be decentralised to the district level and decided in consultation with the Zilla panchayats. Total homework time determined in there is (i) No homework up to Class II and two hours a week from Class III of primary schools, (ii) One hour a day (about five to six hours a week) Middle school, and (iii) Two hours a day (about 10 to 12 hours a week) in Secondary and Higher Secondary.

In new pedagogical practices, all these changes necessitate the teachers' training to enable them to achieve new goals and objectives. The NCF has presumed the new roles and responsibilities for the teachers and made numerous suggestions for their training. Teacher education programmes need to be reformulated and strengthened so that the teacher can be an encouraging, supportive and humane facilitator in teaching-learning situations to enable learners to discover their talents, to realise their physical and intellectual potentialities to the fullest, to develop character and desirable social and human values to function as responsible citizens. For ensuring a learning environment, teacher autonomy and professional independence are essential that cater to diverse needs of learners.

In the process of knowledge construction, shared context of learning, teacher as a facilitator of knowledge construction, multidisciplinary nature of knowledge of teacher education, integration of theory and practice dimensions, and engagement with issues and concerns of contemporary Indian society from a critical perspective, such teacher education programmes place thrust on the active involvement of learners.

In this context, in teacher education and an integrated model of teacher education centrally of language proficiency for strengthening professionalisation of teachers, assume significance. As a catalyst for change in school practices, the NCF 2005 perceives in-service teacher education.

Q21. Explain the concept and need of Universalisation of Elementary Education (UEE).

Ans. Universalisation of Elementary Education (UEE) is an educational term refers to make education available to all children in the age of group of 6-14 years or in classes I-VII. It means education for every child to complete the stage of Elementary or Primary education either formal or non-formal means of education. Here all children covered the children of every community castes, creed, religions, handicapped, orphans or destitutes and disadvantaged groups. In short, universalisation of elementary education is the educational provision for all children to educate elementary education without any dropouts. As per Article 45 of the Constitution of India, Provision for free and compulsory education for children- The State shall endeavour to provide, within a period of ten years from the commencement of this Constitution, for free and compulsory education for all children until they complete the age of fourteen years.

The base of all types of human development and progress is education. In the absence of education, human life becomes meaningless. Education is said to be the sharpest weapon and strongest shield against all human problems. India is a democratic country and justice, equality and liberty are the guiding principles of our Constitution. To deprive someone of the right of obtaining education is a gross injustice, and hence, in a democratic and secular country like ours universalisation of at least primary education is of prime importance.

Universalisation of education implies five things namely, universalisation of provision, universalisation of enrolment, universalisation of retention universalisation of participation and universalisation of achievement.

Universalisation of Elementary Education (UEE) has been accepted as a national goal in India since Independence. The founding fathers of our Constitution recognised UEE as a crucial input for nation building. UEE is also a Constitutional directive.

At the time of Independence, India inherited a system of education which was not only quantitatively small but also characterised by structural imbalances. Only fourteen per cent of the population was literate and only one child out of three had been enrolled in primary school. The low levels of participation and literacy were aggravated by acute regional and gender disparities. As education is vitally linked with the totality of the development process, the reform and restructuring of the educational system was recognised as an important area of state intervention.

The need for a literate population and universal education for all children in the age group of 6-14 was recognised as a crucial input for nation building and was given due consideration in the Constitution as well as in successive Five Year Plans.

Q22. Discuss the reasons for non-achievement of goals of universalisation of elementary education as mentioned in Article 45 of the Constitution of India.

Ans. Article 45 of the Indian constitution provides for free and compulsory education to children in the age group 6-14 years. UEE was part of all five years plans. Government, non-government agencies, voluntary organizations and private organizations are engaged in this task but goal to provide education for all still remains.

Following are the reasons for non-achievement of goals of UEE:

(1) **Unemployment:** Many parents don't want to send the children to schools because they think that as educated youth are unemployed. However, this view is not correct and to change this type of negative attitude a teacher have to work hard.

(2) **Dropouts, wastage and stagnation:** If the children are enrolled in the schools, they dropout due to various reasons. In completion of education of children upto the elementary level, the wastage and stagnation are big barriers.

(3) **Poverty:** For thousands of parents sending the children in school is a luxury which they cannot afford. Their children had to work hard for earning livelihood. Hence, they don't get their children enrolled in schools. They do engage their children in many types of work.

(4) **Lack of awareness and ignorance:** Ignoring the value of education is curse. In our society, many of the parents don't realise the importance of education in human life and it is only out of ignorance they don't get their children enrolled in the schools.

(5) **Gender bias:** The rate of women literacy is lower than that of male literacy in many Indian states. Here, gender bias is predominant in many societies. It is observed that education is imparted to male child while education of female child is neglected. Instead she has to shoulder the responsibility of helping her mother in routine work.

(6) **Lack of Stability in life:** Some tribes and nomads are still homeless and they have to wander from place to place in search of livelihood. Some laborers' also lack stability in life. Many children are orphans. We can imagine that in all such cases taking education becomes a distant dream.

(7) **Communication gap:** There exists a big communication gap between the Govt. agencies and people in remote, hilly and tribal areas. The children living in these areas don't have easy access to education. Local agencies and NGOs are also not in a position to cater for education in such problematic areas.

(8) **Agriculture based economy:** India is agriculture based economy and due to poverty and in absence of modern technology, the parents prefer to engage their children to work in the fields instead of send them to schools.

(9) **Lack of motivation:** Today, the Indian government gives incentives to the school-going children such as free education,

scholarships and other facilities, but still proper motivation is lacking among parents to send their children to the school.

(10) Population-explosion: In spite of quantitative expansion and network of schools, education could not reach the doorsteps of each and every child in the country. The rate of development lagged behind the rate of growth of population. Fast growth of population has created many problems in all walks of our life.

Q23. State the provisions made in the 86th Constitutional Amendment (2002).

Ans. The Constitution 86th Amendment Act, 2002 enshrined right to education as a fundamental right in part-III of the constitution. Be it enacted by Parliament in the Fifty-third Year of the Republic of India as follows:

(1) This Act may be called the Constitution (Eighty-sixth Amendment) Act, 2002. It shall come into force on such date as the Central Government may, by notification in the Official Gazette, appoint.

(2) A new article 21A was inserted below the Article 21 which made Right to Education a Fundamental Right for children in the range of 6-14 years. This article reads: "The State shall provide free and compulsory education to all children of the age of six to fourteen years in such manner as the State may, by law, determine"

(3) Article 45 which originally stated: "The State shall endeavour to provide, within a period of ten years from the commencement of this Constitution, for free and compulsory education for all children until they complete the age of fourteen years." Was substituted as "The State shall endeavor to provide early childhood care and education for all children until they complete the age of six years."

(4) Article 51A was also amended and after clause (J), the clause (k) was added which says: "who is a parent or guardian to provide opportunities for education to his child or, as the case may be, ward between the age of six and fourteen years."

Q24. Discuss about Right to Education Act, 2009.

Ans. The Right of Children to Free and Compulsory Education Act or Right to Education Act (RTE), is an Act of the Parliament of India enacted on 4 August 2009, which describes the modalities of the importance of free and compulsory education for children between 6 and 14 in India under Article 21a of the Indian Constitution. India became one of 135 countries to make education a fundamental right of every child when the Act came into force on 1 April 2010.

The Act makes education a fundamental right of every child between the ages of 6 and 14 and specifies minimum norms in elementary schools. It requires all private schools to reserve 25% of seats to children (to be reimbursed by the state as part of the public-private partnership plan). Kids are admitted in to private schools based on economic status or caste based reservations. It also prohibits all unrecognised schools from practice, and makes provisions for no donation or capitation fees and no interview of the child or parent for admission. The Act also provides that no child shall be held back, expelled, or required to pass a board examination until the completion of elementary education. There is also a provision for special training of school dropouts to bring them up to par with students of the same age.

The Right to Education of persons with disabilities until 18 years of age is laid down under a separate legislation - the Persons with Disabilities Act. A number of other provisions regarding improvement of school infrastructure, teacher-student ratio and faculty are made in the Act.

Education in the Indian constitution is a concurrent issue and both centre and states can legislate on the issue. The Act lays down specific responsibilities for the centre, state and local bodies for its implementation. The states have been clamouring that they lack financial capacity to deliver education of appropriate standard in all the schools needed for universal education. Thus, it was clear that the central government (which collects most of the revenue) will be required to subsidise the states.

Q25. Discuss the various features of CRC. What are the Child Rights under UN Convention?

Or

Describe the rights of the child as given in the United Nation's Convention on Rights of the Child.

Ans. The most important international legal instrument for protection of child rights is the UN Convention on Child Right (CRC). It focuses on the human rights for children because they are a vulnerable group and need special guidance from adults and their protection. The various features of CRC are as follows:

(i) Applies to both girls and boys upto the age of 18, even if they are married and have children of their own.

(ii) The convention is guided by the principles of 'Best Interest of the Child' and 'Non-discrimination' and 'Respect for the views of the child'.

(iii) It emphasizes the importance of the family and the need to create an environment that is conducive to the healthy growth and development of the children.

CRC draws attention to four sets of civil, political, social, economic and cultural rights. These are:

- Survival
- Development
- Protection
- Participation

There are some of the important child rights as follows:

- All people under the age of 18 are entitled to the standards and rights guaranteed by the laws that govern our country and the international legal instruments we have accepted by ratifying them.
- The Constitution of India guarantees all children certain rights, which have been specially included for them. These include:
- Right to free and compulsory elementary education for all children in the 6-14 year age group (Article 21 A).
- Right to be protected from any hazardous employment till the age of 14 years (Article 24).
- Right to be protected from being abused and forced by economic necessity to enter occupations unsuited to their age or strength (Article 39(e)).
- Right to equal opportunities and facilities to develop in a healthy manner and in conditions of freedom and dignity and guaranteed protection of childhood and youth against exploitation and against moral and material abandonment (Article 39 (f)).

Q26. Explain the roles and responsibilities of the teacher in implementing the provisions of the Right to Education Act, 2009.

Or

Mention any one role of the teacher under RTE Act.

[April-2016, Q.No.-19]

Or

Explain the role and responsibilities of the teachers to achieve the goal of cent percent literacy.

[October-2016, Q.No.-19]

Ans. In the RTE Act, all teachers are expected to perform the following roles and responsibilities:

- Performing only the prescribed duties by teacher may not help to achieve the goals of RTE. Teacher should rather emerge as great supporters of RTE and work as an active agent for the effective implementation of the provisions of RTE Act 2009.
- Complete the entire curriculum within the specified time.
- Assess the learning ability of each child and accordingly supplement additional instructions, if any, as required.
- Maintain regularity and punctuality in attending school.
- A teacher's responsibility to extend all types of help to make the child free of fear, trauma and anxiety, they should

implement carefully the procedure of comprehensive and continuous evaluation (CCE). Teachers have to make all efforts to build up child's knowledge, potentiality and talent and work for development of his/her physical and mental abilities. In short, they are expected to bring about the all round development of the child.

- Hold regular meetings with parents and guardians and apprise them about the regularity in attendance, ability to learn, progress made in learning and any other relevant information about the child.
- Perform such other duties as may be prescribed.

Q27 Write short notes on the following:

(i) School Governance and Management

Ans. The importance of governance and management of the school should never be forgotten. Unless a school is managed in a proper way, teachers will not be able to achieve the goals of RTE. There are many provisions in RTE regarding proper arrangement and governance of the school. According to the Act, no school shall be established or recognised unless and until it fulfills all the norms and standards for imparting education effectively. It means the school must have necessary infrastructural and educational facilities.

The first teacher of a child is mother, we will appreciate the provision that the management committee of school will consist of at least 50% women and most of the office bearers and members of this committee will be from parents' category. There are following functions the Management committee is expected to perform:

- Monitor the grants received from various sources.
- Work for the mission of achieving the goals of RTE.
- Monitor the working of school.
- Prepare and recommend the school development plan.

It is joint responsibility of teachers and management of the school to ensure that all eligible children get enrolled in the school and continue to attend the school till they complete elementary education.

(ii) Curriculum and Evaluation Imperatives

Ans. At this stage, the curriculum is expected to develop minimum basic skills and attitudes in the children. It will be child-centered and related to day-to-day life of the child. It should be flexible enough to accommodate the needs and requirements of children of different abilities and belonging to varied Socio Economic Status. It is expected to be inclusive and flexible enough, to cater to the requirements of children with special needs. Curriculum will be constructed in conformity with the values enshrined in the RTE Act. It should be helpful in building up child's knowledge, potentiality and talent. The curriculum should promote learning through activities and there should be spacious scope for games and sports and organisation of the co-curricular activities.

Till the completion of elementary education of the child, there shall be no external examination, all children are to be promoted to higher class but this does not mean that teacher should neglect the evaluation part. A scheme of comprehensive and continuous evaluation (CCE) is to be implemented. Teacher will have to be very careful regarding quality of education. Though there is no pass and fail system, in any case the standard of education should be maintained. To bring about all round development of the child is the main aim of education. It is teacher responsibility to build up the child's knowledge, potentiality and talent. Teacher should take every care to inculcate favourable attitudes and positive values of life in the children. Teacher should also promote various skills, learning through activities and spirit of discovery. To develop physical and mental abilities of children teacher's should try their best to the fullest extent.

Q28. What are the Model Rules? Discuss the details that the RTE Model Rules document comprises.

Ans. The Model Rules, 2009 on the Right to Education Act have been formulated to help operationalise the Act. These rules provide a broad framework which the different states could use while devising their own State Rules on RTE. The Model Rules document in its current form lays down details on:

- Method and details of records to be maintained of children within the jurisdiction of a local authority.
- Documents as age proof required for every child
- Teacher qualifications norms.
- Application and procedure to be followed by all schools 'other than a school established, owned or controlled by the State Government or Local Authority' in order to gain recognition as mandated by the Act.
- Details on the school development plan to be designed and monitored by the SMC.
- Provisions and methods special training of children in order to bring them up to the learning level of their peers
- Conditions and procedures under which this recognition could be withdrawn.
- Duties of the state govt. and local authorities in up-gradation of schools, provision of transport facilities, or residential facilities and all forms of learning support to children with disabilities to ensure completion of elementary education.
- The limits of neighbourhood schools
- Composition and function of the school management committee.
- Responsibilities of schools and teachers with regard to enrollments and classroom transactions with children from weaker sections and disadvantaged groups.

Q29. Analyse the important rules for free and compulsory education of child.

Ans. The important rules for free and compulsory education of child are divided into eight parts:

(I) PRELIMINARY

In these rules, unless the context otherwise requires:

(a) "Act" means the Right of Children to Free and Compulsory Education Act, 2009.

(b) "Anganwadi" means an Anganwadi Centre established under the Integrated Child Development Scheme of the Ministry of Women and Child Development of the Government of India

(c) "appointed date" means the date on which the Act comes into force, as notified in the Official Gazette

(d) "Chapter", "section" and "Schedule" means respectively Chapter, section of, and Schedule to, the Act.

(e) "Child" means any child of the age of 6 to 14 years

(f) "Pupil Cumulative Record" means record of the progress of the child based on comprehensive and continuous evaluation

(g) "school mapping" means planning school location to overcome social barriers and geographical distance

(II) RIGHT OF CHILDREN TO FREE AND COMPULSORY EDUCATION

Special Training for the purposes of first proviso to section 4

The School Management Committee/local authority shall identify children requiring special training and organise such training in the following manner, namely:

(a) The special training shall be based on specially designed, age appropriate learning material, approved by the academic authority.

(b) It shall be provided in classes held on the premises of the school, or through classes organised in safe residential facilities.

(c) It shall be provided by teachers working in the school, or by teachers specially appointed for the purpose.

(d) The duration shall be for a minimum period of three months which may be extended, based on periodical assessment of learning progress, for a maximum period not exceeding two years.

(III)DUTIES OF STATE GOVERNMENT, LOCAL AUTHORITY

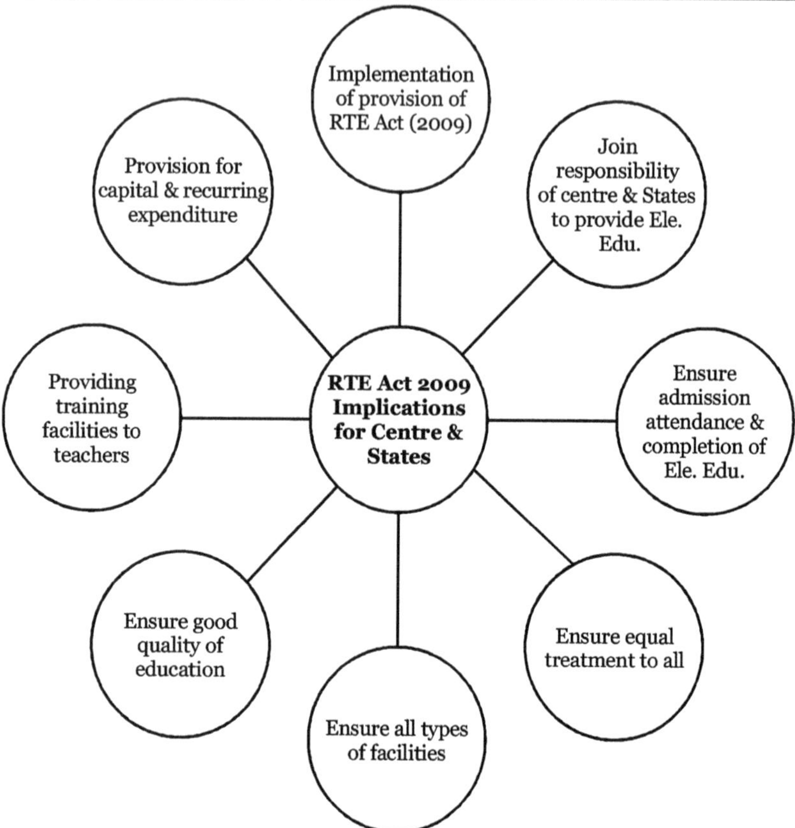

Fig. 1.2: Duties of state government

(1) The areas or limits of neighbourhood within which a school has to be established by the State Government shall be as under:

   (a) In respect of children in classes I - V, a school shall be established within a walking distance of one km of the neighbourhood.

   (b) In respect of children in classes VI - VIII, a school shall be established within a walking distance of 3 km of the neighbourhood.

(2) Wherever required, the State Government shall upgrade existing schools with classes I - V to include classes VI – VIII. In respect of schools which start from class VI onwards, the State Government shall endeavour to add classes I – V, wherever required.

(3) In areas with difficult terrain, risk of landslides, floods, lack of roads and in general, danger for young children in the approach from their homes to the school, the State

Government/Local Authority shall locate the school in such a manner as to avoid such dangers, by reducing the limits.

(4) The Local Authority shall identify the neighbourhood school(s) where children can be admitted and make such information public for each habitation within its jurisdiction.

Maintenance of records

(1) The Local Authority shall maintain a record of all children, in its jurisdiction, through a household survey, from their birth till they attain 14 years.

(2) The record shall be updated each year.

(3) The record shall be maintained transparently, in the public domain.

(4) The record shall in respect of every child, include:

(a) name, sex, date of birth, (Birth Certificate Number), place of birth;

(b) parents' / guardians' names, address, occupation;

(c) pre-primary school/Anganwadi centre that the child attends (upto age 6);

(d) elementary school where the child is admitted;

(e) present address of the child;

(f) class in which the child is studying (for children between age 6-14), and if education is discontinued in the territorial jurisdiction of the Local Authority, the cause of such discontinuance;

(g) whether the child belongs to the weaker section within the meaning of clause (e) of section 2 of the Act;

(h) details of children requiring special facilities/residential facilities on account of migration and sparse population; age appropriate admission; disability.

(5) The Local authority shall ensure that the names of all children enrolled in the schools under its jurisdiction are publicly displayed in each school.

(IV) RESPONSIBILITIES OF SCHOOLS AND TEACHERS

Every school, other than a school established, owned or controlled by the State Government or Local Authority shall help to implement the provisions of RTE. The school is not run for profit to any individual, group or association of individuals or any other persons. The role of District Education Officer is very important because he is expected to act as custodian to implement the provisions of RTE Act in an effective way. The schools shall work under instructions of DEO. Teachers have to play a pivotal role in the Universalisation of Elementary Education (UEE) because in implementation of the RTE Act, they are supposed to be main human resource.

(V) SCHOOL MANAGEMENT COMMITTEE

A School Management Committee shall be constituted in every school, other than an unaided school, within its jurisdiction, within six months of the appointed date, and reconstituted every two years. As per provision of the RTE Act, the School Management Committee shall be constituted mainly out of parents of children and their strength shall be 75%. Some of the important functions of the committee will be as follows:

- There shall be a grievance redressal mechanism for teachers. The State Government shall constitute School Tribunals at the State, District and Block levels.
- The State or local authority shall maintain the pupil teacher ratio.
- Monitor that the teachers are not burdened with non-academic duties (except with those of census and elections)
- In addition to normal duties, the teachers are required to maintain a file containing the cumulative record of every child which will form the basis for awarding the completion certificate to the concerned child for that particular year. We are expected to participate in training programmes, curriculum formulation, training modules, and textbook development.

(VI) TEACHERS

The academic authority shall within three months of such notification, lay down the minimum qualifications for persons to be eligible for appointment as a teacher in an elementary school. The minimum qualifications laid down by the academic authority shall be applicable for every school.

(VII) CURRICULUM AND COMPLETION OF ELEMENTARY EDUCATION

Academic Authority for the purposes of section 29

(1) The State Government shall notify the State Council of Educational Research and Training (or its equivalent), as the academic authority for the purposes of section 29.

(2) While laying down the curriculum and evaluation procedure, the academic authority notified under sub-Rule (1) shall (a) formulate the relevant and age appropriate syllabus and text books and other learning material (b) develop in-service teacher training design, and (c) prepare guidelines for putting into practice continuous and comprehensive evaluation

(3) The academic authority referred to in sub-rule (1) shall design and implement a process of holistic school quality assessment on a regular basis

Award of certificate for the purposes of section 30

(1) The Certificate of completion of elementary education shall be issued at the school/block/district level within one month of the completion of elementary education.

(2) The Certificate referred to in sub-rule (1) shall:

(a) certify that the child has completed all courses of study prescribed under section 29.

(b) contain the Pupil Cumulative Record of the child and also specify achievements of the child in areas of activities beyond the prescribed course of study and may include music, dance, literature, sports, etc.

(VIII) PROTECTION OF RIGHTS OF CHILDREN

In respect of a State which does not have a State Commission for Protection of Child Rights, the State Government may take immediate steps to set up the Commission. Till such time as the State Government sets up the Commission, it shall constitute an interim authority known as the Right to Education Protection Authority (REPA). All records and assets of the REPA shall be transferred to the State Commission for Protection of Child Rights immediately after its constitution.

Q30.What are the various types of children's rights?

Or

Describe the various types of children's right categorised by a Canadian organization.

Or

Analyse any two areas of children's rights as categorised by a 'Canadian organisation'. [October-2016, Q.No.-33]

Ans. Children's rights tend to be of two general types: those advocating for children as autonomous persons under the law and those placing a claim on society for protection from harms perpetrated on children because of their dependency. These have been labeled as the right of empowerment and as the right to protection.

A Canadian organisation has categorised the children's rights into three categories:

- **Protection:** Protection stands for the right to be shielded from certain acts and practices (social and individual misuses). These rights include protection from all forms of child abuse, neglect, exploitation and discrimination. This includes the right to safe places for children to play; constructive child rearing behavior, and acknowledgment of the evolving capacities of children.
- **Participation:** Participation stands for the right to do things, express oneself and have an effective voice as an individual child and as a larger group. Children are entitled to participate in communities and have programmes and services for themselves. This includes children's involvement in libraries and community programs, youth voice activities, and involving children as decision-makers.
- **Provision:** Provision refers to sharing and distribution; it includes the right to possess, receive or have access to certain resources and services. These are rights to an adequate standard of living, health care, education and services, and to play and

recreation. These include a balanced diet, a warm bed to sleep in, and access to schooling.

Two groups are categorises by the Child Rights Information Network, or CRIN:

- **Cultural, economic and social rights**, related to the conditions necessary to meet basic human needs such as food, shelter, education, health care, and gainful employment. Included are rights to education, adequate housing, food, water, the highest attainable standard of health, the right to work and rights at work, as well as the cultural rights of indigenous and minorities people.
- **Cultural, development and environmental rights**, also known as "third generation rights," and including the right to live in safe and healthy environments and that groups of people have the right to cultural, political, and economic development.

Scholarly study generally focuses children's rights by identifying individual rights. The following rights "allow children to grow up healthy and free":

(i) Freedom from fear

(ii) Freedom of speech

(iii) Freedom of thought

(iv) Ownership over one's body

(v) Freedom of choice and the right to make decisions

Education is in the concurrent list. The joint responsibility of the Central as well as State Governments is to import education. The Central Government and the State Government shall have concurrent responsibility for providing funds for carrying out the provisions of RTE Act.

- The State Government, from the funds received from the Central Government and its own resources, for the implementation of the provisions of RTE will be responsible to provide funds.
- The Central Government shall provide to the State Government, as grants-in-aid of revenues such percentage of expenditure as it may determine, from time to time, in consultation with the State Government.
- It shall be the joint responsibility of the Central Government & the concerned State Government to provide free elementary education to every child of the age of 6 to 14 years. Here, it is not easy to meet the huge expenditure to be incurred for providing education to all. It is going to be the biggest challenge to for this task spare thousands of crores of rupees.
- For the implementation of the provisions of RTE Act the Central Government shall prepare the estimates of capital and recurring expenditure.

The concerned State Government will have to:

- Ensure that no discrimination is made on any ground among children regarding persuasion of elementary education.
- Ensure that quality elementary education is accessible to every child. Teachers are important in maintaining the quality of elementary education.
- Ensure the availability of all types of infrastructural and educational facilities to each and every child for completion of elementary education. Many a times in want of financial support, good infrastructural facilities are not provided.
- Provide training facilities to those teachers who are working in the area of elementary education.
- Ensure compulsory admission attendance and completion of elementary education by every child.
- Ensure availability of neighborhood school.

Q31. What do you mean by National Council of Educational Research and Training (NCERT)? Discuss its aims and major constituent units.

Or

When, where and how was the National Council of Educational Research and Training established?

[October-2016, Q.No.-35]

Ans. NCERT is an apex resource organisation set up by the Government of India, with headquarters along Sri Aurobindo Marg in New Delhi, to assist and advise the Central and State Governments on academic matters related to school education. It was established in 1961 at Delhi.

Qualitative improvement and excellence in school education and teacher education are some of its major objectives. To achieve them, the NCERT undertakes programmes related to research, development, training, extension and dissemination of educational information through its constituent departments - the CIET, the regional colleges of education at Ajmer, Bhopal, Bhubaneswar and Mysore and 17 field offices located all over the country.

The NCERT continues to coordinate and monitor activities related to the UNICEF- assisted projects in elementary and non-formal education and UEFPA- assisted National Population Education Project (school and non-formal education). The NCERT maintains effective liaison with state education authorities and state level institutions for providing academic inputs to the school education system.

During 1992-93, the major achievements of NCERT were directed towards early-Childhood Care and education (ECCE), Universalisation of Elementary Education (UEE), Minimum Levels of Learning (MLL), orientation of content and process of education at the school stage, improvement of science education in school, computer literacy, vocationalisation of education, teacher education, education of SCs/ STs and minorities, education for women's equality, education of disabled children, utilisation of educational technology, educational survey and data processing, National Talent Search Scholarship, promotion of educational research and publication of textbooks for CBSE affiliated schools in the country.

NCERT develops curricula and syllabi and prepares textbooks for classes I-XII. The syllabi prepared by NCERT form the basis for prescription of schemes of studies by Central Board of Secondary Education (CBSE) for the students of schools affiliated to the Board. It develops instructional material for childhood education and training packages for teacher educators and supervisory personnel. The council produces science kits for the use of school students. It prepares comprehensive guidelines for curriculum evaluation and schoolindustry linkages as well as for pre-service and in-service education of teachers on vocationalisation of education. Training courses for the officials involved in the integrated education programme for disabled children are also conducted by the NCERT.

There are four aims of NCERT as follows:

- To spread the education.
- To solve educational problems faced by school education in the country
- To organise the training Programmes.
- To improve the quality of school education

The major constituent units of NCERT which are located in different regions of the country are:

- National Institute of Education (NIE), New Delhi
- Central Institute of Educational Technology (CIET), New Delhi
- Pandit Sundarlal Sharma Central Institute of Vocational Education (PSSCIVE), Bhopal
- Regional Institute of Education (RIE), Ajmer
- Regional Institute of Education (RIE), Bhopal
- Regional Institute of Education (RIE), Bhubaneswar
- Regional Institute of Education (RIE), Mysore
- North-East Regional Institute of Education (NERIE), Shillong

Q32. Examine the role and functions of NCERT.

Ans. Role of NCERT

- To monitor the administration of NIE / Regional colleges of Education.
- To undertake aid, promote and co-ordinate research in all branches of education for improving school – education
- To organize pre-service and in-service education programmes for teachers.
- To prepare and publish study material for students and related teacher's handbooks.

- To search talented students for the award of scholarship in science, Technology and social sciences.
- To undertake functions assigned by the Ministry of education (Now HRD) for improving school –education.
- To promote, organize and foster research in all fields of education.
- To disseminate knowledge of improved educational techniques and practices; and
- To conduct special studies, surveys and investigations.

Functions of NCERT

(1) **Research:** Independently or in collaboration with other organisations, undertakes research in the field of education.

(2) **Training:** It organises pre-service and in-service training of teachers in such areas as vocational education, educational technology, guidance and counseling and special education, and also at various levels; pre-primary, elementary, secondary and higher secondary.

(3) **Development:** It updates and develops curricula and instructional materials /syllabi for various levels of school education and makes them relevant to the emerging needs of society. It develops educational technology including educational aids and evaluation procedures and techniques.

(4) **Pre-service and in-service training:** It organise pre-service and in-service education programmes for teachers teacher educators and other education personnel.

(5) **Orientations:** It organises orientation to those concerned with school education and teacher education regarding new educational thoughts, ideologies and information in all subjects.

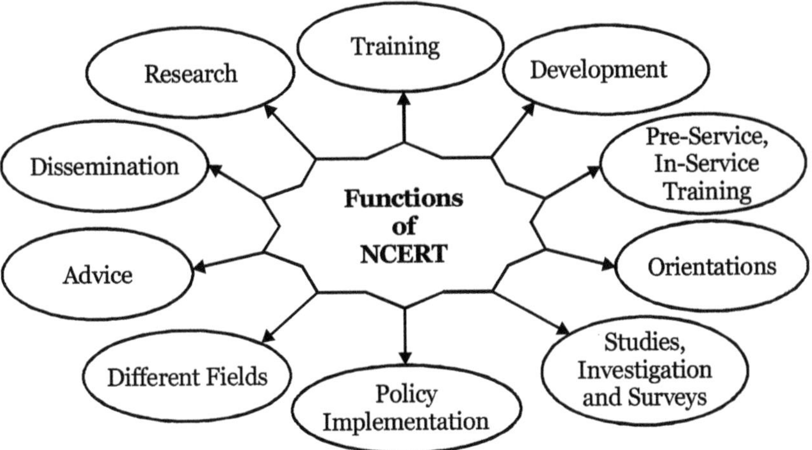

Fig. 1.3: Functions of NCERT

(6) **Studies, Investigation and Surveys:** It undertakes and organises studies, investigations and surveys relating to educational matters.

(7) **Dissemination:** It disseminates improved techniques and practices.

(8) **Advice:** It advises the Centre and the States as well as other academic institutions in matters pertaining to school education.

(9) **Policy Implementation:** In addition to dealing with specific development and research activities on its own initiative, it undertakes the implementation of the policies and programmes of the Ministry.

(10) **Different fields:** It deals with specific problems in different fields like curriculum, textbooks, publication, examination, etc. and undertakes research in these fields with a view to improving the quality of education at school stage.

Today, NCERT coordinates with international agencies working in school education. International agencies are working with NCERT on various projects like UNESCO, UNICEF, World Bank, etc.

Q33. Explain the term 'SCERT'. Also discuss its organisational structure.

Ans. The State Council of Education Research and Training (SCERT) is also known as SIE in some states. It came into existence on 5 January 1979 by the transformation and upgradation of the former State Institute of Education (SIE). It provides academic guidance to the Regional Officers, District Education Officers, Block Education Officers and Principals of Schools. SCERTs are headed by Directors and under them are Joint Directors of different sections like Curriculum Development, Textbooks Production Division, Non-Formal Education, Science and Maths Division, Integrated Education for Disabled Children, Population Education, etc.

Organisational structure of SCERT: Working for specific purposes, SCERT has various departments:

- Department of Curriculum Development
- Department of Teacher Education and in-Service Education
- Department of Educational Research
- Department of Science and Mathematics Education
- Department of Educational Technology
- Department of Evaluation and Examination Reforms
- Department of Non-formal Education
- Department of Population Education
- Department of Pre-school and Elementary Education

SCERT has other departments, such as:

- Accounts Department
- Publication Department

- Academic Cell
- Administration Cell

Q34. Describe the roles and functions of State Council of Education Research and Training (SCERT).

Ans. Roles of SCERT

The roles of SCERT are as follows:

(1) It controls and supervises the working of the Secondary Training Schools, DIETs, Training Colleges, Colleges of Teacher Education and Institutes of Advanced Studies in Education.

(2) The SCERT arranges monitors and provides funds for inservice training for primary and secondary school teachers. Such programmes are conducted through CTE, IASE and DIET.

(3) It studies the curriculum at primary level, revises it and produces suitable learning materials on different subjects at the primary level keeping in view the MLL in those subjects.

(4) It provides extension service to teacher training institutions, and co ordinates the work of all extension service centers

(5) It implements schemes and projects sponsored by MHRD, NCERT and funded by international agencies such as UNESCO, UNICEF, World Bank, etc.

(6) It also develops learning package for pre-school children.

(7) It orients teachers about the MLL, and strategies to be followed to help children achieve MLL in different subjects.

(8) The SCERT is the academic wing of the State Education Department on matters of elementary education, secondary education and teacher education.

(9) It acts as an agent of change in school education, non-formal education and teacher education.

(10) It conducts research studies on various aspects of school education. It also provides financial assistance to schools for research projects.

(11) It sends proposals for appointment and transfer of teachers, teacher educators and heads of teacher training institutes.

Functions of SCERT

The State Council of Educational Research and Training discharges the following functions:

(1) Pre-service and in-service training: For development of skills in teachers, it conducts teacher training programme and other training programmes.

(2) Guidance: It provides guidance like for continuous and comprehensive evaluation, standard learning patterns, pedagogy, portraying effective learning methods, etc. to schools/teachers on various innovative practices.

(3) **Curriculum revision and review of textbooks:** For primary and upper primary classes, the most important function of the SCERT is curriculum revision and review of textbooks.

(4) **Orientations:** In various areas, it organises orientation programmes for empowerment of teachers such as the proficiency enhancements, research aptitude, leadership behaviour, etc.

(5) **Total quality management:** The focus of total quality management on the total quality management (TQM) concept; it tries to remove the root causes of the quality problems, rather than treating its symptoms.

(6) **Conduct the workshops:** It conducts workshops on research methodologies focusing on different areas of competencies.

Q35. Discuss about 'SIEMAT'. Explain the roles of SIEMAT.

Ans. The SIEMAT (State Institute of Educational Management and Training) is established in various states to support the educational planning, management, conduct and evaluation studies and provides professional support through various capacity building programmes in these fields. It is an apex institute in the area of educational planning, management, research, evaluation, counselling and capacity building of educational planners, executors, supervisors and the supporting staff.

Roles of SIEMAT: Roles of SIEMAT will be to impart Educational Management Training to all Administrative Officers and functionaries involved in management of school education. The roles of the SIEMAT are as follows:

(a) Provide technical support to educational institutions

(b) Capacity to absorb knowledge and use it for developmental purposes e.g.

- Extension work.
- District and micro level planning,
- Orientation of functionaries, trainers, community leaders,
- Render professional and technical advice,
- Improving school effectiveness - institutional planning,

(c) Acquisition of knowledge

- Compilation of case studies based on the national and international experiences.
- Generation of knowledge through research,
- Research findings from other sources,

(d) Dissemination of knowledge through
- Sensitisation sessions,
- Seminars and discussions.
- Use of media,
- Publications,

Q36. What are the functions of SIEMAT?

Ans. The major functions of SIEMAT are as follows:

(a) Competency development of Educational Managers, their supporting functionaries and community leaders of State, Region and district levels

(b) To document and disseminate, Block, District, State, National and International level information in the area of educational planning and other aspects of management.

(c) Providing a sharing platform for those involved in educational planning & management.

(e) To offer on request consultancy services to other States, Government of India and other educational institutions.

(f) Support to NGO projects for furthering the cause of educational planning and management.

(g) Conduct research studies on various aspects

(h) Develop and manage system of evaluation of educational institutions, educational programmes as well as prevalent systems of education.

(i) Support in project planning, implementation, monitoring and evaluation.

(j) Support to policy planning at the state level.

(k) Developing local level capacities

(l) (Professional guidance to State and Sub-State level institutions

(m) Providing support, guidance and training for behavioral change of functionaries.

(n) To establish a network within and outside the State for educational planning, management development, monitoring, training and research.

Q37. What is District Institutions of Education and Training (DIETs) and what are its functions?

Ans. District Institute of Education and Training (DIET) is a nodal agency for providing academic and resource support at the grass-root level for the success of various strategies and programmes undertaken in the areas of elementary and adult education. With special reference to Universalisation of Primary/Elementary Education and National Literacy Mission (NLM) targets with regards to functional literacy in 15-35 age group. DIETS are the special institutions established with the special aim of improving primary education.

Functions of DIET: The official DIET guidelines (MHRD 1989) expected them to pursue key functions:

(1) Training and orientation of the following target groups

(a) elementary school teachers;

(b) Head Masters, officers of Education Department up to Block level;

(c) NFE and adult education instructors and supervisors;

(e) Meembers of District Boards of Education and Village Education Committees, other community volunteers;

(f) Resource persons who will conduct suitable programmes at the centres other than the DIET.

(2) Academic and resource support to the elementary and adult education systems in the district through:

(a) Extension activities and interaction with the field,

(b) Provision of services of a resource and learning centre for teachers and instructors,

(c) Development of locally relevant materials, teaching aids, evaluation tools etc., and

(d) Serving as an evaluation centre for elementary schools and programmes of NFE/AE.

(3) Action research and experimentation: To deal with specific problems of the district in achieving the objectives in the areas of elementary and adult education.

In order to activate the DIET to discharge these functions, additional physical facilities (such as building, etc.) instructional materials, aids and equipment, additional, competent and qualified teacher educators, autonomy, training to the personnel and financial grants are provided to DIETs. In addition to these, new branches have been created in the DIET such as the following:

(1) Pre-Service Teacher Education (PSTE) Branch organises two-year Diploma course in Elementary Teacher Education (ETE). The course prepares trainees to provide learner-centered education and education for over all development of personality of learners including children of disadvantaged group i.e. first generation learners and children with major handicaps and other mild handicaps also. The branch provides input into programmes and activities of all other branches of the institutes to the extent of subjects and areas represented/handled in the branch.

(2) Work Experience (WE) Branch identify locally relevant WE areas and develop sample curricular units, teaching material, low cost teaching aids and evaluation tools.

(3) **Curriculum, Material Development and Evaluation Branch (CMDE)** to serve as a centre for providing support in the area of development of local specific curriculum and materials, and evaluation for elementary schools as well as for AE / NFE centres at district level.

(4) **District Resource Unit (DRU)** focuses on planning, implementation, co-ordination, monitoring, evaluation and training of AE/NFE//NGOs personnel throughout the district and provides necessary support to such programmes organised outside the institute. The unit undertakes action research in all areas relevant for making AEINFE more effective in collaboration with other branches of DIETs. The unit coordinates UEE mission activities in the district, monitors, supervises the learning centers, provides academic resource support to the learning centres, and conducts training of the teachers of learning centers.

Q38. Discuss the structure and roles of DIET.

Ans. Structure of DIETs: In order to facilitate suitable structure to implement the innovative concept of DIET, seven academic branches have been suggested:

- Pre-Service Teacher Education (PS-TE)
- Work Experience (WE)
- District Resource Unit (DRU)
- In-service programmes, Field Interaction and Innovation Co-ordination (IFIC)
- Curriculum, Material Development and Evaluation (CMDE)
- Educational Technology (ET)
- Planning and Management (P&M)

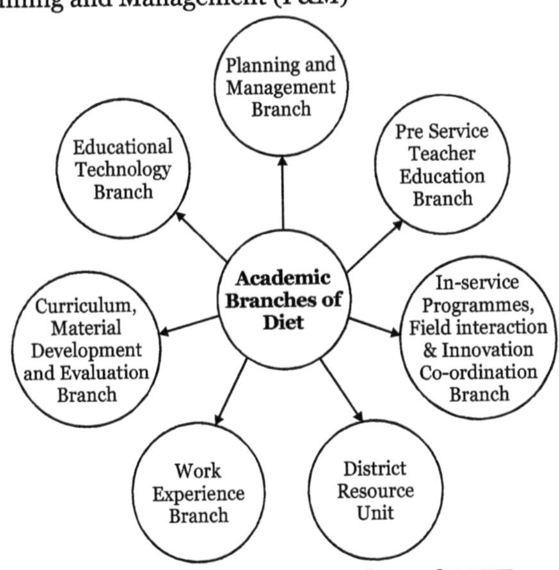

Fig. 1.3: Academic branches of DIET

Role of DIET

DIET performs the following main role:

- to train teacher, research workers in conducting action research and to provide resource support to them,
- to share research findings, to incorporate those in district plans for further improvement in respective interventions,
- to design and conduct minor research studies on various aspects of elementary education,
- to monitor the action research activity in the district,
- to identify problem areas through direct interaction with different stakeholders of the district and sub-district levels.

Q39. What do you know about Block Resource Centres (BRCs). Explain the roles and functions of BRCs.

Ans. BRC is a Block level institution to carry out the academic activities related mainly to primary education. BRC carries out its academic programmes under the guidance and supervision of DIET. Every BRC should have a vision shared with the vision of the DIET at the District level. BRCs comprise a group of 100 villages. Block Education Officer co-ordinates the activities of a BRC with technical support of other personnel like data entry operators, junior engineers, block coordinators, resource teachers and other personnel.

Roles and Functions of BRCS: There must be involvement of BRC in planning, implementing and monitoring SSA activities. It gives training to teachers, Develops material, Community mobilisation, action research works and organisation of different activities/competitions among teachers and students. Any information on primary education is completed by BRC and subsequently made available to district and State level officials. BRC seeks to be a resource centre for giving all kinds of onsite academic support to the elementary school teachers. The functions of BRCs are following:

(a) Conducting periodical review meetings with other officials of the block to remove any bottleneck in the execution of the various programme inputs.

(b) Supervising the training programmes at the blocks and assessing the impact of the training.

(c) To secure the co-ordination and co-operation of other agencies like, NGOs, SHG (self-help groups), Government Departments, etc.

(d) To monitor the progress and quality of construction of educational works undertaken in the block.

(e) To organise awareness campaigns and block-level functions.

(f) To be responsible for the enforcement of compulsory attendance within its area,

(g) To arrange wherever possible, midday meal to children

(h) To provide uniform to children and

(i) To celebrate school functions and to organise excursions and other social and cultural programmes in the school

(j) To provide adequate accommodation and equipment to primary school

(k) To exercise such supervision over the school as may be prescribed

(l) To carry out current repairs of school buildings and if authorised also to carry out special repairs and to construct new buildings.

Q40. What do you mean by Cluster Resource Centres (CRCs)? Also discuss the roles and functions of CRCs.

Ans. Cluster Resource Centers have been functioning as Centers of teacher empowerment, where the teachers share their experiences and innovative practices in the teaching learning processes. The monthly CRC meetings have been primarily used for sharing innovative practices in classrooms by the teachers.

Roles of CRCs: The following are the roles of CRCs:

(i) To arrange workshops for teachers,

(ii) To manage and distribute school's finances,

(iii) To make arrangements for implementing new curriculum/ syllabus,

(iv) To prepare rules and procedures for school's functioning.

Functions of CRCs: The functions of CRCs broadly include:

(i) Training at cluster level

(ii) Follow-up and support visits to schools (sharing problems, lesson demonstration, etc.)

(iii) Collecting data and information asked for by BRC (enrollment, attendance, dropout, etc.)

(iv) Holding meetings with VEC members

(v) Providing support to activities undertaken at CRC level

(iv) Undertaking activities that build environment

(iiv) Making CRC a resource centre (equipping with books, discussion paper, etc.)

(iiiv) Collecting information about civil works

(ix) Feedback to BRC

(x) Attending monthly meetings at BRC

CRC have been involved in conducting training programmes for Teachers. In some states, they have supervisory powers. In the monthly meetings all the CRC Teachers come together to share and discuss their academic and administrative problems. One of the major activities at these meetings has been lesson demonstration followed by discussions. The CRC Coordinator facilitates the discussions and sometimes gives lesson demonstrations also. A coordinator, who is normally a primary school Teacher with 10-15 years of experience, heads a CRC. The main aim of GPH book is provide knowledge as well as good marks in Exam.

Objective Type Questions

Q1. The first Committee to be constituted after independence by the Government of India on Women's Education was

(A) Dr. Radhakrishnan Commission

(B) The Mudaliar Commission

(C) The Shri Sri Prakasa Committee

(D) Dr. Durgabai Deshmukh Committee

Ans. (D) Dr. Durgabai Deshmukh Committee

Q2. District Institute of Education and Training are established for:

(A) Pre-service Training of Teachers

(B) Training for SSA personnel

(C) Consolidation of Block Resource Centres

(D) All of the above

Ans. (D) All of the above

Q3. SIEMAT performs the function of dissemination of knowledge through:

(A) compilation of case studies

(B) institutional planning

(C) seminars and discussions

(D) technical support

Ans. (C) seminars and discussions

Q4. Operation Black-Board Programme was introduced to improve:

(A) Teacher Education

(B) Primary Education

(C) Secondary Education

(D) Higher Education

Ans. (B) Primary Education

Q5. Which one of the following is not a salient feature of the National Policy on Education, 1986?

(A) Military training for national defence

(B) Promotion of adult education

(C) Equal educational opportunities for all

(D) Accountability to education

Ans. (A) Military training for national defence

Q6. The right to free and compulsory education for children between age group of 6 to 14 has been inserted in Indian Constitution as:

(A) Article 46

(B) Article 16

(C) Article 45A

(D) Article 21A

Ans. (D) Article 21A

Q7. Education can accelerate the process of modernisation by:

(A) raising the salaries of teachers

(B) emphasising teaching of vocational subjects and science

(C) introducing common school system of public education

(D) presenting before students high ideas of social justice

Ans. (B) emphasising teaching of vocational subjects and science

Q8. The meaning of Universalisation of Primary Education is to provide:

(A) Education to all

(B) Education to all girls children

(C) Free and compulsory education to all children

(D) Free and compulsory education to the children of 6 – 14 years age

Ans. (D) Free and compulsory education to the children of 6 – 14 years age

Q9. The University Grants Commission was constituted on the recommendation of:

(A) Dr. Sarvapalli Radhakrishnan Commission

(B) Mudaliar Commission

(C) Sargent Commission

(D) Kothari Commission

Ans. (A) Dr. Sarvapalli Radhakrishnan Commission

Q10. 10+2+3 system of education was recommended by:

(A) Kothari Commission

(B) Mudaliar Commission

(C) Radhakrishnan Commission

(D) National Policy on Education (1986)

Ans. (A) Kothari Commission

Q11. The purpose of National Education Policy is:

(A) Universalisation of primary education

(B) Vocationalisation of education

(C) To review the education

(D) To give equal opportunity of education to all

Ans. (C) To review the education

Q12. The in-service teacher' training can be made more effective by:

(A) Using training package which in well prepared in advance

(B) Making it a residential programme

(C) Using co-operative approach

(D) Practicing training follow up procedures

Ans. (D) Practicing training follow up procedures

Q13. The aim of education should be:

(A) To develop vocational skills in the students

(B) To prepare the students for practical life

(C) To prepare the students for examination

(D) To develop social awareness in the students

Ans. (B) To prepare the students for practical life

Q14. The purpose of new education policy is:

(A) To provide equal opportunity of education to all

(B) To improve the whole education system

(C) To link the education with employment

(D) To delink the degree with education

Ans. (B) To improve the whole education system

Q15. 'National Council of Educational Research and Training' was established in:

(A) 1961

(B) 1962

(C) 1963

(D) 1964

Ans. (A) 1961

Q16. At primary level, it is better to teach in mother language because:

(A) It develops self-confidence in children

(B) It makes learning easy

(C) It is helpful in intellectual development

(D) It helps children in learning in natural atmosphere

Ans. (D) It helps children in learning in natural atmosphere

Q17. In ancient India religions and moral aims were dominated by:

(A) Brahmnic system of education

(B) Kshatriya system of education

(C) Both A & B

(D) None of the above

Ans. (C) Both A & B

Q18. When was National Policy on education formulated?

(A) Aug, 1986

(B) Jan, 1986

(C) March, 1988

(D) Oct, 1988

Ans. (A) Aug, 1986

Q19. Macaulay wrote his famous minute on educational policy on___?

(A) 16th February

(B) 8th February

(C) 1st February

(D) 2nd February

Ans. (D) 2nd February

Q20. Higher education was given during Vedic Period in:

(A) Gurukuls

(B) Charan

(C) Shakhas

(D) All above

Ans. (D) All above

Q21. Which Commission recommended the induction of applied science and technology in the University Course?

(A) Mudaliar Commission

(B) Sadler Commission

(C) Hunter Commission

(D) Indian University Commission

Ans. (B) Sadler Commission

Q22. During Vedic Age pupil were called:

(A) Brahamana

(B) Brahmachari

(C) Charka

(D) None of these

Ans. (B) Brahmachari

☺☺☺

GULLYBABA PUBLISHING HOUSE PVT. LTD.

ISO 9001 & 14001 CERTIFIED CO.

First Year

Course-501: Elementary Education in India: A Socio-Cultural Perspective

Course-502: Pedagogic Processes in Elementary Schools

Course-503: Learning Languages at Elementary Level

Course-504: Learning Mathematics at Elementary Level

Course-505: Learning Environmental Studies at Primary Level

Second Year

Course-506: Understanding children in inclusive context

Course-507: Community & Elementary Education

Course-508: Learning in Art, Health & Physical and Work Education at Elementary Level

Optional

Course-509: Learning Social Science at Upper Primary Level

Course-510: Learning Science at Upper Primary Level

Elementary Education in India in the Cotemporary Context-I

INTRODUCTION

Education is a concern of both the state and the central governments. The state governments have been providing education in India since independence. The central government also launched many sponsored programmes in 1986 through the National Education Policy (NEP) which improved the status of elementary education in the country. To achieve the goal of universalisation of elementary education different strategies have been emphasised through different project like UP Basic Education Project, Bihar Education Project for improving the quality of primary education, Lok Jumbish for Girls education and Shiksha Karmi for teacher absenteeism. Sarva Shiksha Abhiyan is a major campaign for achieving universal elementary education in the country. SSA has been designed to provide elementary education to children in the age group of 6-14 years. Government is making efforts also in bringing all children in school with disability, SC, ST children, children belonging to minority section of our society, children of migrant families and working children, etc.

Q1. Discuss the various aspects of UEE.

Ans. Three aspects of Universalisation of Elementary Education (UEE) are as follows:

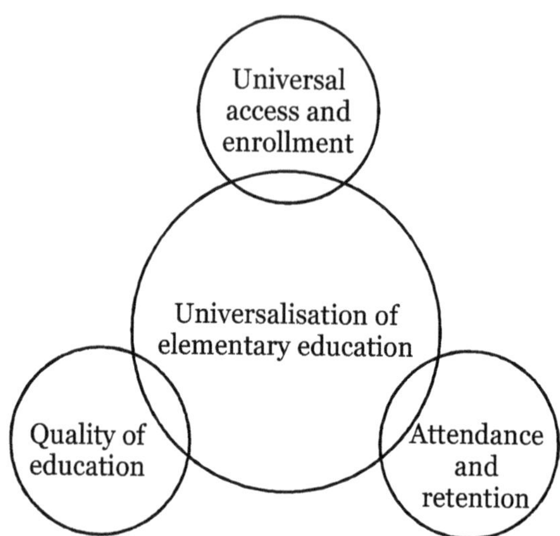

Fig. 2.1: Aspects of UEE

(1) **Universal access and enrollment:** Availability of schooling facilities is measured by a set of indicators concerning to access. Recently, it is planned by Indian government to set up a primary school at every kilometer for easy access to the students. A survey of the families which come under the jurisdiction of that particular school is made in the starting of the year by that school. A list of eligible children for education as well as those who are out of schools is made, in order to bring both of them to the school. After opening of school, an enrollment week is observed to ensure 100% enrollment of all eligible students.

(2) **Attendance and retention:** To retain the disadvantaged children enrolled in school is so far a more challenging task than enrolling them into the educational system itself, so universal retention of children up to the 14 year of age is a must. Therefore, many facilities like daily attendance allowance, free travelling pass, free mid-day meal etc. are provided and new techniques of teaching are adopted to improve the attendance.

(3) **Quality of education:** The last but the most important aspect of UEE is the Quality of Education that is measured in India in terms of learner's achievement. Even, the states that have almost attained universal access, enrolment and retention, the quality of education is very poor. It is only in the recent past (during 1990's) that quality of education has got attention of policy makers. It may be noted that India

follows policy of no detention up to primary level i.e. IV/V. But in practice, divergent models are in existence across states. Generally, at the end of primary cycle, examinations are compulsory and promotion to next cycle is linked to children performance in this examination.

Q2. Elucidate the following project mode for universalisation of elementary education:

(i) Uttar Pradesh Basic Education Project (UPBEP)

Ans. The Uttar Pradesh Basic Education Project was the first major primary education project funded by the World Bank in India. A project "Education for All" prepared by the Government of Uttar Pradesh was approved by The World Bank in June, 1993. It was planned to expand the coverage to 15 districts under DPEP-II. It had an outlay of ₹7,288 million spread over seven years. International Development Agency (IDA), the soft loan window of The World Bank, would provide a credit of US$ 163.1 million and the State Government's share would be approximately 13 per cent of the total project cost.

Objectives of the Project: Objectives of the project were as follows:

- Universal achievement programme for minimum level of learning.
- Universalization of P.E. viewed as a composite programme of Access to P.E for all children up to 14 years of age, and universal participation till they complete primary level through formal and non-formal education.
- Equal education opportunity to SC and ST children.
- In education, female empowerment and greater gender equality.
- Provision of education and skill development programme for youth.

Strategies: Following strategies were adopted in the project:

- Quality of education was used to improve by early childhood education curriculum and textbook revision, In-service training, women & girl education and strengthening school management.
- Strong framework of State and district level planning, management and professional support state organisation was established to build the institutional capacity to plan, manage and evaluate different basic education development programmes.
- Improving access to basic education in ten districts by constructing more primary & upper primary schools in deprived areas and supporting redesigned implementation of non-formal education for out of school children.

Activities: The following activities were focused:

- Science & environment.
- Educational activities on culture and communication.
- Creating a sense of social justice

Implementation: Project's different activities were concentrated in 10 targeted districts out of 63 districts of Uttar Pradesh including Uttaranchal. These districts were Varanasi, Allahabad, Banda, Etawah, Sitapur, Aligarh, Saharanpur, Gorakhpur, Pauri and Nainital.

(ii) Bihar Education Project (BEP)

Ans. The Bihar Education Project is a basic education project aims to bring about qualitative improvement in the educational system and through it, in over-all socio-cultural situation in the state. It comprises all components of basic education. Almost all educational indicators in Bihar were negative, i.e. there were lowest enrolment ratios and highest dropout rates in the century.

Large-scale teacher absenteeism degraded educational infrastructure, mismanagement of adult and non-formal education programmes and general administrative apathy before the project.

Bihar Education Project represents the first major attempt in India to include the broad range of national EFA concerns, issues, approaches and strategies in one large-scale operational programme. This project launched in 1991 jointly by the view of primary education.

Apart from teachers, trainees included District Superintendents of Education (DSEs) and Block Education Officers (BEOs). The main objective was to orient teachers to the importance of primary education, gender issues, depressed classes, their participation and also preparation and use of teaching-learning materials using resources for their

immediate environment, and making classroom transactions childcentered.

Objectives: Objectives of the project were as follows:

- Primary education, as a composite programme of universal success, universal participation and universal achievement (nearer to the minimum levels of learning);
- Modification in the educational system to serve the objects of equality for women and their empowerment;
- Inculcating equality and social justice in educational endeavours;
- To increase enrollment capacity of the education and reduce dropout especially of girls and SC students.
- Laying special emphasis on all educational activities on science and environment.

Strategies: Following were the strategies of the project:

- Recruitment of about 16,000 additional teachers
- Training of the newly recruited teachers
- Implementation of Mahila Samakhya component
- Construction of about 11,000 primary and upper primary classrooms.
- Participatory planning and implementation
- Provision of the materials to the newly opened schools.

Activities: Project took the following activities:

- Non-formal education through NGOs.
- At the grass root level, organisation of Village Education Committees and community involvement in the programme implementation.
- Organisation of state level workshop: Training of key persons and primary teachers for minimum level of learning is given
- Mahila Samakhya: To establish local accountability of the schools, to play an active role in management of ECCE and NFE centers, support teachers and participate in VEC.
- Enrolment drives
- Constitution of core group at district level for women's development
- Introduction of computerized monitoring system for education sector.
- Poster workshop: expansion of the concept of rural libraries, etc.

Implementation: Management structures establishment at State\District level, women empowerment, extensive community mobilisation, mobilisation of greater national/international interest in basic education, etc. Selection of classrooms – on the basis of analysis of populations and enrollment problems village level micro plans has been decided. Project supervision –this would be twice a year in conjunction with the supervision of UPBEP I and second District Primary Education Project.

Q3. What is meant by Lok Jumbish? What are its objectives and components?

Ans. An innovative project called "Lok Jumbish" (People's movement for Education for All) with assistance from Swedish International Development Authority (SIDA) has been undertaken in Rajasthan. The basic objective of the project is to achieve education for all by the year 2000 through people's mobilisation and their participation. The girls and women's education were the major thrust areas. During the first phase of the project in 1992-94, Lok Jumbish covered 25 blocks spread over several districts with an expenditure of ₹14.03 crores shared by SIDA, Government of India and Government of Rajasthan in the ratio of 3:2:1. The Second phase of Lok Jumbish project was implemented between 1994-97. In this phase, the project was extended to 50 blocks. An outlay of ₹80 crores was shared by SIDA, GOI and GOR in the ratio of 3:2:1. The third phase of the project commenced, in July 1999, with the assistance of DFID, UK, GOI and GOR on a sharing pattern.

Objectives: The major objectives/aims of the Lok Jumbish are as follows:

(1) Providing access to primary education to all children upto 14 years of age through the school system as far as possible and part-time non-formal education where necessary;

(2) Ensuring that all enrolled children attend school/NFE centre regularly and complete primary education;

(3) Ensuring that quality of education is improved by emphasising active learning, child-centred processes and achievement by all children at least up to the minimum levels of learning;

(4) Creation of necessary structures and setting in motion processes which would empower women and make education an instrument of women's equality;

(5) To pursue the goal of equity in education between boys and girls and between the socially and educationally disadvantaged sections and the rest of the society and also to initiate measures for provision of basic education to the handicapped children;

(6) Making necessary modifications in the content and process of education to better relate it to the environment, people's culture and with their living and working conditions; and

(7) Effectively involve people in the planning and management of education.

Main Components: Following are the main components of this project:

- School mapping and micro planning represent the principal operational feature of Lok Jumbish at the village level, carried out by social animators, teachers and Lok Jumbish functionaries for assessment of education which help to track progress of each child by his\her name.
- Creation of autonomous body for launching and managing programmes with an empowerment of committee which will review progress.

Q4. Discuss the strategies and activities of Lok Jumbhish Project.

Ans. Strategies of Lok Jumbish Project was as follows:

(1) Adhyapika Munch was created for getting participation of women.

(2) Developed a mechanism at bottom level like Prerak Dal, Bhavan Nirman Committee, Village education Committee, Cluster, Khand Stariya Shiksha Prabandhan Samiti (block level mgt) and Block steering groups to support and monitor programmes as a period of trial in five blocks.

(3) Review planning meetings (RPMs) of all functionaries at cluster and block level was held in every month to review work and plan for next month and the same process was repeated at state level with 2-3 RPMs.

(4) Increased the number of functionaries at all levels to start matrix system of management to fulfill their responsibility of working area.

(5) Praveshotsav is an event through which a positive and creative environment created for education amongst children, the school and the community.

The main activities undertaken in this project are given in the following figure:

Hostels for tribal's children	• To cater the educational needs of children of seasonal migrants as well as those living in remote habitat
Mahila Shikshan Vihar	• Residential courses for out of school girls in 15+ age group have been conducted here which provide quality education in a residential type of atmosphere in rural areas.
Balika Shikshan Shivir	• Residential camp of 6 to 8 months of school for girls in 9+ age group to facilitate reentry to formal education
Muktangan	• It was a programme for tribal children's in Khandela Cluster of Kishanganj block in Baran
Madrassa	• Strengthening to reach to children from minority communities in Kaman block of Bharatpur.
Institutionalisation of Sahaj Shiksha Kendra	• It is a non-formal education programme to cater to the needs of working children.
School health programme	• This programme is focussing on efforts to generate awareness among the school children
Anganwadi centers	• For the strengthening the programme of pre-primary education and its linkages with primary education NGO 'Vihan' promoted by UP has taken up 245 Anganwadi centres

Fig. 2.2: Main Activities of Lok Jumbish

Q5. Define Shiksha Karmi Project. What are its objectives?

Or

List any four objectives of the Shikshakarmi Project.

[October-2016, Q.No.-36]

Ans. Shiksha Karmi project (SKP) is being implemented in Rajasthan since 1987 with assistance from the Swedish International Development Agency (SIDA). The project aims at Universalisation and Qualitative improvement of primary education in remote and socio-economically backward villages in Rajasthan with primary attention being given to girls. The project identifies teachers' absenteeism as a major obstacle in achieving the objective of UEE. The project is being implemented by the Govt. of Rajasthan through Rajasthan Shiksha Karmi Board (RSKB) with the assistance of voluntary agencies. During the first phase from 1987 to 1994, 90% of the project outlay was funded out of the plan budget of the Central Government, which was subsequently reimbursed by SIDA.

Objectives of the project: Following are the objectives of Shiksha Karmi Project:

(1) Universalisation of primary education in remote, socio-economically backward villages in those blocks of Rajasthan where the existing primary schools have been dysfunctional.

(2) A qualitative improvement of primary education in such villages by adapting the form and content of education to local needs and conditions.

(3) Improvement in enrolment of all boys and girls in the age group 6-14 years.

(4) Building of a level of learning equivalent to the norms of Class V.

(5) To overcome major problem of poor enrolment and high dropout of children, particularly girls.

(6) Making necessary interventions to provide equal educational opportunity to - adults and children belonging to the lower castes, ethnic communities and poorest section of society.

Q6. Enumerate the strategies, implementation and activities of Shiksha Karmi Project.

Ans. Strategies

Strategies of the Shiksha Karmi project are given as follows:

(1) Evolved a procedures based on field experiences and consensual decision-making.

(2) A Monitoring Mission commissioned by SIDA held on Bi-annual review of the Shiksha Karmi Project.

(3) Promoted gender and social sensitivity in access.

(4) Greater decentralisation and more community involvement.

Implementation: Rajasthan Government and non-governmental organisations work hand in hand with the Project Director to design, organise and conduct training for SK trainers and oversee training of Shiksha Karmi.

To fulfill the needs of the rural areas deprived sections, education services must have support of the Panchayat Samiti, Shiksha Karmi Sahayogi, and Subject Specialist of non-Govt. organisations, Shiksha Karmi and the village community to achieve the aims of the project.

Activities : *Integrated approach*—A survey has revealed that 6% of children up to 14 years of age in the Blocks Ghatol (Tribal) and Balotra (Desert) suffer from physical disabilities so scheme to integrate disabled children in SKP schools was established.

Day Centre—When the existing primary schools run by Shiksha Karmi, it is called Day centre.

Prehar Pathshalas—The children who can't attend day centres they come to schools at night, it is called Prehar Pathsalas.

Mahila Prakashan Kendra—The project also lays emphasise on recruitment of female Shiksha Karmi and establishment of Mahila Karmi training centre is called as Mahila Prakashan Kendra. It prepares local women to work as Mahila Shiksha Karmi.

Q7. Give brief description on the following schemes under the projects for primary education which have been invented by the government of Maharashtra:

(i) Schemes for socially Deprived Children

Ans. Socially backward classes are enlisted as Schedule cast, Schedule tribes, Nomadic caste and tribes. For the welfare of backward class boys and girls of Maharashtra, State Government runs following projects:

- Free uniform and book
- National Board of talent research established by NCERT gives scholarship after completing secondary Education to SC & ST
- Stipend up to 10th class
- Book bank Scheme
- Boarding houses
- Ashram schools
- Hostel for government and private agencies
- Allowance for attendance.

(ii) Schemes for Girls

Ans. For family as well as for society, girls' education is very important. Many projects for girls' education have been started by the state.

- **Free travelling scheme for girls by Ahilyabai Holkars:** To promote education among girls, the state government has started Ahilyabai Holkar scheme, providing free travel concession to girl students from 1996-97. Under this scheme, girls in the rural areas studying in standards V to X are provided travel in Maharashtra concession to attend the school through State Road Transport Corporation. About 14.44 lakh girls availed such facility under this scheme.
- **Army School:** The government started army school at Bhor at Nasik to encourage the girls of Maharashtra. Girls are also provided some stipend as well as opportunity for further training if they are physically fit.
- **Allowance for attendance:** All the girls from backward classes are given one rupee per day as allowance if they are

present for 75% working days in the school and this has been done to reduce the dropouts in STD I–IV.

- **Samuh Nivasi School:** Samuh Nivasi Schools are opened because the girls from remote areas unable to reach school due long distance.
- **Matruprabodhan Project:** In the rural area, to achieve the aim of universalisation of primary education, programme has been arranged to educate mother about children education, their health and personal development.

(iii) Schemes for Economically Backward Children

Ans. Many people are economically weak in every caste and religion in society. They could not send their children to school for education. Due to poverty, these children has to work leaving school and start earning for the family.

Following are some schemes for these children:

- **E.B.C:** This project was started by the Government of Maharashtra from 1956. Students with 75% attendance & passed every year with yearly income of ₹15000/- of parent will be awarded by this scholarship.
- **Savitribai Phule Parent Adoption Scheme:** This scheme was started in 1993. Due to financial condition, many girls leave schools. According to this scheme Principal, Officers and any member of the society can adopt any of these girls and give the help of minimum thirty rupees every month up to 7th Std.
- **Scholarship:** This scholarship was started by the Government of Maharashtra in 1978 to talented and economically backward students of higher secondary level in which ₹70/ will be given to boys and ₹80 to girls.
- **Book bank Scheme:** Primary schools' students are getting school books free of cost. The books are taken back after one year and when the New Year starts the activity is repeated. The Students of I & II std are provided new books par year. All the books of higher classes in the book bank can be exchanged with new books.
- **Nutritive Diet:** Village development committee started this project in 1995. Every child who is attending school regularly is provided with nutritive diet in recess.

(iv) Schemes for Distant Area Children

Ans. In 1970, many schemes were started by the Govt. of Maharashtra to educate the children living in remote (deep) areas:

- **Ashram Shala:** The plan of Ashram Shala was implemented by the directorate of tribal development. Because of poverty in remote areas parents unable to complete the needs of their children. These poor children enrolled in ashram schools for literacy, lodging and uniform free of cast. These schools run class from Std I to X and also supervised by administration. There are two types of Ashram Shala– Basic Ashram Shala for Std I to VII and Para Basic Asharam Shala for Std V to X.

- **Vidya Niketan:** For talented tribal students, it is the Ist institute installed in Kelapur, Yavatmal district in 1981. The students were given free education. For girls, independent Vidya Niketan is also established. 10 seats are reserved for adivasi students in all educational institutes.
- **Child Education Project:** Under UNICEF, Maharashtra state started this project in 1982. The books are provided to the children full of different pictures to increase their interest in books and schools. Parent meeting are also organised to make them assure of their wards progress.
- **Kuranshala:** It is mobile school imparting non-formal education. The implementation of first Kuranshala was by Smt. Tarabai Modak and Smt. Anutai Wagh. Teacher has to follow the students to the forest areas and teach them informally about cleanliness, medicines, good habits, language and try to develop their standard of life.
- **The Project for Tribal Languages:** Language of schools and language of tribal areas, both are different to each other. So it is a difficult for tribal children to understand standard language. To remove this difficulty, both languages must be similar so that the students may be acquainted with mother tongue as well provincial language. So MSCERT prepare the text books in tribal languages for these children and also prepare hand book for teachers along with the training.
- **Nutritive Diet Scheme:** The aim of this scheme is to improve the standard diet of the children in 0–6 years of age. The nutritive diet is provided to children of Anganwadi & Balwadi. The children of schedule tribe also get benefit of this scheme and show mental & physical development. Mid-day meal is also provided to student of STD I to V.

(v) Schemes for Out of the School Children

Ans. Many students are deprived from education due to poverty. Government has installed many projects to bring them back in formal education.

- **Bridge School:** Bridge courses during vacation offering remedial lessons to children left behind due to irregular attendance and seasonal migration of families. After completion of this period of about 45 days they are sent for admission in the regular primary and Sec. Schools. This school is boarding house come school having syllabus of 45 days only. The children left studies gathered here & taught according to their classes in which they studied & then they send to regular school. The person who run this type of school are HSC passed and try hard so that these children may regularly attend bridge school.

According to the needs of bridge school and students government also prepares syllabus and books.

- **Indus Child Labour Project:** As a child labour, many children are working in different profession. This scheme aim to root out the child labour tradition and bring them to main stream of education. This project is implemented in five districts of Maharashtra viz. Gondia, Amravati, Jalana, Aurangabad & Mumbai. MS CERT has taken responsibilities to train volunteers of this project. This child labour project has been organised nationally through the society known as National child labour project (N.C.L.P).
- Only with accommodation of at least 50 students, the center must be open within the locality. In the centre, students of different age groups will be there so while teaching group system should be applied to make it easy for student. It should be considered that student are coming after working so different programmes should be organised and different teaching aids should be used to increase their interest in studies.
- **Sakhar Shala:** In the settlements of sugar cane cutters, Sakhar Shala schools are opened, which intend to provide primary education to children of sugarcane laborers. Because of parent's migration to the factory areas on a regular basis, or for long periods their children are deprived of education as there is no special provision for migrant children to continue their education at factory sites Sakhar Shala try to solve problems in continuing education by opening schools and providing adequate educational services in settlements of migrant laboures.
- **Cape Project:** In 1981, for the out of school children of age 6-14 years, Maharashtra Government in assistance with UNICEF started this project called primary Education for all. Self-learning center opened attached to the education colleges where 25-30 out of school children get admitted & they come to school according to their convenience for part time Classes.
- **Remedial Teaching Classes:** The students from bridge school, M. Phule Hami Yojana remains deprived in studies because of their low concentration. These classes help students to reach minimum level of learning.
- **Vastishala:** These are mostly primary schools imparting informal education in hilly, tribal and remote areas where there is no school within a radius of one Km. and the syllabus of classes 1-4 be taught to the students. A minimum 15 students of classes from 1-4 should be enrolled for starting a vasti-schools in premises allotted by Gram Panchayat. Village Education Committee arranges for the qualified teachers and 30 days training is also given by DIET, prior to joining school.

(vi) The Scheme for Special Target Group (Handicapped, Devdasi Children, etc.

Ans. Children included in this group are belonged to different social strata and castes, religion and educationally backward class. These children could not complete primary education. Therefore, they are given special attention under some schemes:

(1) **Schemes for children of Devdasi:** It is a negative social tradition. Due to blind faith many Devdasis are still socially and economically backward hence cannot give education to their children. Therefore, some schemes have been started for children of Devdasis and Varangana.

- Book bank Yojana
- Nutritional meal
- Women's Probodhan program
- Attendance allowance.
- Free pass Yojana
- Boarding schools-Snehalaya

(2) **Education for handicapped:** Integrated education is approachable for these children. In it, open learning methods through which non-formal education, Distance Education, Moving schools, remedial education and part time education, vocational Education etc. are included.

(3) **Education for disabled children:** Special schools have also been started by Maharashtra government for disabled children. In 1885, a deaf & dumb school was established in Mumbai. But supposed if these children are given a chance to similar to general children, their self confidence will improve hence they are being admitted to general school. This is called integrated approach.

Q8. What is DPEP (District Primary Education Project)? Explain its objectives and major components.

Ans. The Centrally-Sponsored Scheme of District Primary Education Programme (DPEP) was launched in 1994 as a major initiative to strengthen the primary education system and to achieve the objective of universalisation of primary education. DPEP adopts a holistic approach to universalise access, retention and improve learning achievement and also to reduce disparities among social groups. Adopting an 'area-specific approach' with district as the unit of planning, the key strategies of the programme have been to retain the sensitivity to local conditions and ensuring full participation of the community. It also seeks to strengthen the capacity of national, state and district institutions and organisations for planning, management and professional support in the field of primary education.

Objectives of DPEP: The DPEP was approved with the following objectives:

(1) To reduce differences in enrolment, dropout and learning achievement among gender and social groups to less than five per cent.

(2) To reduce overall primary dropout rates for all students to less than 10 per cent.

(3) To raise the average achievement levels by at least 25 per cent over measured base line levels and ensure achievement of basic literacy and numeracy competencies and a minimum of 40 per cent achievement level in other competencies by all primary school children.

(4) 100% access to education for children in age group of 6 to 14 years through formal or non-formal education.

(5) To provide according to national norms, access to all children to primary education classes (I-V), i.e. primary schooling wherever possible or its equivalent non-formal education.

Major Components of DPEP: Following were four major components of DPEP:

- **Programme:** For providing school facilities to children several alternative approaches could not be brought under the formal system of education are being implemented. DPEP activities are an essential element in the programme.
- **School Mapping and Micro Planning:** The aim of Micro Planning is involving the community in identifying barriers to enrollment and participation in primary education. It also draws community support to find solutions to overcome these barriers. Micro planning helps to fix up the responsibilities by concretising the role of VEC. The educational system of the village is monitored by these VECs and contributed to the progress of enrollment and retention.
- **Civil Works:** DPEP will finance civil works (limited to 24% of project cost) such as construction of new primary schools, new class rooms, major repairs and rehabilitations of schools, construction of toilets, residential schools, rooms at ECCE centres, water supply and electrification, SIEMT, and other state educational facilities as approved by DPEP, Maintenance would be financed as per state norms and be within the 24% ceiling.
- **Management:** Distinct management structures are envisaged by DPEP to facilitate better implementation of the programme, to closely monitor the activities by developing a Management Information System (MIS) and to facilitate faster flow of funds. These structures are envisaged at the national, state and district levels. These new structures are supportive to the district plans and are supposed to get merged with the existing organisational arrangements by the end of the project period.

Q9. Describe execution plan of DPEP. Also, give its strategies and activities.

Ans. The DPEP made a serious effort to translate the idea of decentralisation into an operational practice through various steps:

- The programme attempted to alter the pattern of resource decisions from state level to local levels.
- To academic activities, it tried to provide professional resource support through new organisational arrangements like the BRCs and CRCs.
- The planning process tried to create local level capacity both at the district and sub-district levels.
- District was identified by the programme as the unit for initiating decentralised educational planning.
- Through providing contingency grants of Rs. 2000/- to each school and ₹500/- to every teacher annually.
- The programme attempted to strengthen the planning process to make it more consultative, participatory and transparent.

Strategies and Activities

- **Tribal and Coastal Education:** Enrollment campaign with the help of volunteers and Panchayat, Awareness programme and free supply of Textbooks to tribal children.
- **Access:** In tribal areas, opening new L.P. Schools, Multigrade Learning Centers in remote tribal area and Alternate schools in remote and backward areas. (Tribal & coastal).
- **Quality Improvement:** Recurrent teacher training on activity based pedagogy, onsite support to teachers through the visit of BRC trainers and monthly cluster meetings of teachers, TTC training for potential SC/ST candidates, Supply of teacher support materials such as handbooks, activity banks, etc., Monthly class PTA meetings and Sahavasa camp.
- **Research and Evaluation:** Action Research Programme, Conduct of studies at BRC & District level.
- **Girls Education:** Free Supply of Textbooks to girls, Awareness programme and Teacher sensitation programme.
- **Community Mobilisation:** Creation of Village Education Committee and Formation of Panchayat Monitoring Cell (PMC), training for PMC and Orientation for Parents.
- **Media:** Publishing of Newsletters at District & Block level and District and Panchayat level exhibition.
- **Management Information System (MIS):** Supply of Computers and Dial up networking to all DPEP District & State Project Office, Appointment of System Analyst cum Programmer, Data Entry Operators. In every year, MIS updates the school database. In every month, MIS develops the data of SOE (Statement of Expenditure) and sends the same to SPO (State project office).

- **Planning and Management:** Orientation for school based planning, Annual Plan preparation through participatory process and Meetings of Block Advisory Committees, District Advisory Board and District Implementation Committee.
- **Village Education Register and Retention Register:** Village Education Register is a register which conveys the educational situation of each boy and girl of all families in the village. Retention register is basically to calculate the retention rate of a school or a class that is, how many children continue their studies and how many drop out.
- **Identification and Education of Disabled Children (IEDC):** Identification of disabled children, supply of aids & appliances, training to teachers, orientation for parents and people's representatives.
- **Distance Education:** Teleconference and supply of distance learning material.

Q10. Write the impact of DPEP on UEE.

Ans. A National Management Structure was set up on the lines of NLMA which would oversee the implementing of the programme throughout the country and a situational analysis was conducted to assess the access and retention in DPEP districts, and to compare the performance of DPEP ones in the selected states. The analysis was based on secondary sources of data obtained from the state Directorate of Education and also from the EMIS established under the DPEP.

Some of the findings/observations of the assessment are as follows:

Coverage

District Covered–219 (248 with bifurcated districts)

- Phase I (1994 – Sept. 2001) 42
- Phase II (1996 – Dec., 2002) 80
- Phase III (1998 – March, 2003) 27
- Other phases 70

States Covered 18

Schools

- Schools in the system 3,75,000
- New school added 10,000

Students and Teachers

- Students in the system 513 lakh
- Total no. of teachers 11 lakh

ECE

- ECE center set up 56,124
- Children covered 21 lakh

Alternative Schools (AS)

- AS centers set up 56,124
- Children Covered 21 lakh

Enrollment

GER (including enrolment in EGS & AS) 102 %

NER (including enrolment in EGS & AS) 90 %

Q11. Define Sarva Shiksha Abhiyan Programme (SSA). What are its essential features?

Or

Who launched the Sarva Shiksha Abhiyan and when?

[April-2016, Q.No.-23]

Ans. Sarva Shiksha Abhiyan (SSA) is a programme for Universalisation of Elementary Education covering the entire country, started in 2001. The programme aims to provide useful and relevant elementary education for all children in the 6 to 14 years age group by 2010. It is an initiative to universalise and improve quality of education in a mission made through decentralised and context specific planning and a process based, time bound implementation strategy. The programme lays emphasis for bridging all gender and social category gaps at elementary education level. SSA was initiated in 2001 following recommendations from the state education ministers' conference in 1998. Although the 86th Amendment to the Constitution enacted in 2002 made elementary education a fundamental right, the Right of Children to Free and Compulsory Education Act that operationalised the provision of free and compulsory education was not passed by the Parliament until August 2009.

Essential Features of SSA

(1) Institutional reforms in states;

(2) Sustainable financing in partnership with states (IX Plan 85: 15, X Plan 75:25, After X Plan 50:50);

(3) Community ownership of school-based interventions through effective decentralisation;

(4) Institutional capacity building for improvement in quality;

(5) Community-based monitoring with full transparency in all aspects of implementation;

(6) Community-based approach to planning with a habitation as a unit of planning;

(7) A mainstreaming gender approach;

(8) Focus on the education participation of children from the SC/ST, religious and linguistic minorities, etc.;

(9) Thrust on quality and making education relevant;

(10) Recognition of critical role of teacher and focus on the human resource development needs of teachers; and

(11) Preparation of District Elementary Education Plans reflecting all governmental and non-governmental investments.

Q12. Enumerate and explain aims and objectives of Sarva Shiksha Abhiyan.

Ans. Aims of SSA

(1) To provide useful and elementary education for all children in the 6-14 age group by 2010.

(2) To bridge social, regional and gender gaps with the active participation of community in the management of schools.

(3) To allow children to learn about and master their natural environment in order to develop their potential both spiritually and materially.

(4) To inculcate value-based learning this allows children an opportunity to work for each other's well being rather than to permit mere selfish pursuits.

(5) To realise the importance of Early Childhood Care and education and looks at the 0-14 age as a continuum.

Objectives of Sarva Shiksha Abhiyan

(1) All children in school. Education Guarantee Centre, Alternate School, 'Back-to-School' camp by 2003.

(2) All children complete five years of primary schooling by 2007.

(3) All children complete of elementary schooling by 2010.

(4) Focus on elementary education of satisfactory quality with emphasis on education for life.

(5) Bridge all gender and social category gaps at primary stage by 2007 and at elementary education level by 2010.

(6) Universal retention by 2010.

(7) Promote local need based planning based on broad National Policy norms.

(8) Allow states to formulate context specific guidelines within the overall framework.

(9) Make planning a realistic exercise by adopting broad national norms.

(10) Encourage districts in States and UTs to reflect local specificity.

Q13. Elucidate broad strategies of Sarva Shiksha Abhiyan.

Or

How does SSA make education at the elementary level useful and relevant to the children?

[April-2016, Q.No.-25]

Ans. Following are the broad strategies of the SSA Programme:

(1) Institutional Reforms: The central and the State governments as part of the SSA, will undertake reforms in order to improve efficiency of the delivery system. The states will have to make an objective assessment of their prevalent education system including educational administration, achievement levels in schools, financial issues, decentralisation and community ownership, review of State Education Act, and recruitment of teachers, monitoring and evaluation, status of education of girls, SC/ST and disadvantaged groups and ECCE. Several changes have been already carried out by many States to improve the delivery system for elementary education.

(2) **Sustainable Financing:** Financing of elementary education interventions has to be sustainable, Sarva Shiksha Abhiyan is based on this premise. This calls for a long-term perspective on financial partnership between the Central and the State governments.

(3) **Community Ownership:** Through effective decentralisation, the programme calls for community ownership of school-based interventions through effective decentralisation. This will be augmented by involvement of women's groups, VEC members and members of Panchayati Raj institutions.

(4) **Institutional Capacity Building:** For national, state and district level institutions like NIEPA/NCERT/NCTE/ SCERT/ SIEMAT/DIET; a major capacity building role is conceived by SSA.

(5) **Improvement in quality:** It requires a sustainable support system of resource persons and institutions.

(6) **Improving Mainstream Educational Administration:** For improvement of mainstream educational administration, it is called by institutional development, infusion of new approaches and by adoption of cost effective and efficient methods.

(7) **Community Based Monitoring with Full Transparency:** SSA will have a community based monitoring system. The Educational Management Information System (EMIS) will correlate school level data with community-based information from micro planning and surveys. likewise, every school will be encouraged to share all information with the community, including grants received.

(8) **Habitation as a Unit of Planning:** The work is done by on a community based approach to planning with habitation as a unit of planning. Habitation plans will be the basis for formulating district plans.

(9) **Accountability to Community:** The cooperation is envisaged by SSA between teachers, parents and PRIs, as well as accountability and transparency to the community.

(10) **Priority to Education of Girls:** One of the principal concerns in Sarva Shiksha Abhiyan will be education of girls,

especially those belonging to the scheduled castes and scheduled tribes and minorities.

(11) Focus on Special Groups: In the educational process, there will be a focus on the inclusion and participation of children from SC/ST, minority groups, urban deprived children disadvantaged groups and the children with special needs.

(12) Thrust on Quality: At the elementary level, SSA lays a special thrust on making education useful and relevant for children by improving the curriculum, child-centered activities and effective teaching learning strategies.

(13) Role of teachers: The critical and central role of teachers are recognised by SSA and it also advocates a focus on their development needs. Setting up of Block Resource Centres/Cluster Resource Centres, recruitment of qualified teachers, opportunities for teacher development through participation in curriculum-related material development and exposure visits for teachers are all designed to develop the human resource among teachers.

(14) District Elementary Education Plans: Each district will prepare a District Elementary Education Plan as per the SSA framework, and reflecting all the investments being made and required in the elementary education sector.

Q14. Briefly explain the role of Public-Private Partnership in SSA.

Ans. This true that provision of elementary education is largely made by the government and government aided schools. But there are also private unaided schools in many parts of the country that provide elementary education. Poorer households are not able to afford the fees charged in private schools in many parts of the country. There are also private schools that charge relatively modest fees and where poorer children are also attending. Some of these schools are marked by poor infrastructure and low paid teachers. While encouraging all efforts at equity and 'access to all' in well-endowed private unaided schools, efforts to explore areas of public-private partnership will also be made. The Sarva Shiksha Abhiyan would cover Government, Local Body, and government aided schools, as is the practice under the Mid Day Meal scheme and DPEP. In case private sector wishes to improve the functioning of a government, local body or a private aided school, efforts to develop a partnership would be made within the broad parameters of State policy in this regard. Depending on the State policies, DIETs and other Government teacher-training institutes could be used to provide resource support to private unaided institutions, if the additional costs are to be met by these private bodies.

Q15. What are the financial norms under Sarva Shiksha Abhiyan? Discuss.

Or

Who supports the salary of teachers appointed under the SSA programme? [April-2016, Q.No.-24]

Ans. Following are the financial norms under Sarva Shika Abhiyan:

(1) The assistance under the programme of Sarva Shiksha Abhiyan will be on a 85:15 sharing arrangement during the IX Plan, 75:25 sharing arrangement during the X Plan, and 50:50 sharing thereafter between the Central government and State governments. Commitments regarding sharing of costs would be taken from State governments in writing.

(2) The State governments will have to maintain their level of investment in elementary education as in 1999-2000. The contribution as State share for SSA will be over and above this investment.

(3) The Government of India would release funds to the State Governments/Union Territories only and installments (except first) would only be released after the previous installments of Central government and State share has been transferred to the State Implementation Society.

(4) The support for teacher salary appointed under the SSA programme could be shared between the Central Government and the State government in a ratio of 85:15 during the IX Plan, 75:25 during the X Plan and 50:50 thereafter.

(5) All legal agreements regarding externally assisted projects will continue to apply unless specific modifications have been agreed to, in consultation with foreign funding agencies.

(6) Existing schemes of elementary education of the Department (except National Bal Bhawan and NCTE) will converge after the IX Plan. The National Programme for Nutritional Support to Primary Education (Mid-Day-Meal) would remain a distinct intervention with food grains and specified transportation costs being met by the Centre and the cost of cooked meals being met by the State government.

(7) District Education Plans would inter–alia, clearly show the funds/resource available for various components under schemes like PMGY, JGSY, PMRY, Sunishchit Rozgar Yojana, Area fund of MPs/MLAs, State Plan, foreign funding (if any) and resources generated in the NGO sector.

(8) All funds to be used for upgradation, maintenance, repair of schools and Teaching Learning Equipment and local management to be transferred to VECs/ School Management Committees/ Gram Panchayat/ or any other village/ school level arrangement for decentralisation adopted by that particular State/UT. The village/school-based body may make a resolution regarding the best way of procurement.

(9) Other incentive schemes like distribution of scholarships and uniforms will continue to be funded under the State Plan. They will not be funded under the SSA programme.

Q16. Describe the interventions in Sarva Shiksha Abhiyan.

Or

What is meant by Alternative and Innovative Education (AIE)? [October-2016, Q.No.-24]

Ans. Interventions in SSA are as follows:

(1) AIE: One of the major interventions of SSA is alternative and innovative education (AIE) which provides access for all children to primary education. Various strategies have been developed for ensuring participation of children of marginalised and deprived groups in tribal and coastal areas.

(2) Civil Works: SSA states the objective of access of Education to every child with in an approach of 1 Km. in Distt. Kaithal under DPEP there have been a war footing approach to provide the schooling facility to each child within these specific limits of 1 Km., but still it requires some Civil Work to be done. So that the infrastructure of every school (Pry. & Upper Pry,) could be better enough according to the educational requirement of every child. Moreover, DPEP has not covered upper pry. Section for any activity. Hence, almost 33% share of total cost of perspective plan of SSA for Distt. Kaithal has been proposed to be laid out for the construction of new school building, new classrooms, boundary walls, toilets, water facilities, maintenance and other infrastructure items.

(3) Innovative activities: The innovative programmes implemented in schools are acting as a catalyst in the process of achieving useful and relevant elementary education for all children in 6-14 age groups and to bridge social, regional and gender gaps in the active participation of the community. These programmes are successful in creating interest among students in education and helped to retain their studies. Early Childhood Care and Education, Girls Education, SC/ST Education and Computer Education, these are the schemes implemented under Innovative schemes.

(4) Research, Evaluation, supervision and monitoring: Research, evaluation, supervision and monitoring are consisted in this intervention. There are provisions for regular school mapping/micro planning for updating of household data. The funds can be utilised for both government and government aided schools. Activities proposed under the intervention are as follows:

(i) Providing regular generation of community based data

(ii) Setting up special task force for low female literacy districts and for special monitoring of girls, SC, ST etc.

(iii) Creating a pool of resource persons for effective field based monitoring

(iv) Conduct cohort studies.

(v) Undertaking contingent expenditure like charts, posters, sketch pen, OHP pen etc. for visual monitoring systems

(vi) Conducting achievement test, evaluation studies

(vii) Incurring expenditure on Education Management Information System

(viii) Undertaking research activities

(5) **School grant:** Under the project, school grant at ₹2,000 each was given. Out of the school grant ₹1000 was given for improvement of school library facilities. The rest money is utilised towards making the non-functional equipment functional, school beautification, repair and maintenance of furniture, musical instruments and over all environment development of schools.

(6) **Teacher grant:** Grant ₹500 is given to each teacher in order to improve the classroom transactions and preparation of teaching aids. The teachers utilised the grant to produce and procure Teacher Learning Material (TLM) for effective classroom transactions.

(7) **Teacher training:** The objective of SSA is undoubtedly the universalization of education. Therefore, along with the SSA, enrolment, retention, we should not forget the most essential element i.e. the quality in education. Teacher is one who is really responsible for providing quality in education. S/he can provide it by using various new techniques or methods. To be well trained & qualified SSA provides teacher training to all trained, untrained & newly recruited teachers.

There is a provision to thoroughly train master trainers orient them to the different issues and concerns of UEE, who will in turn train his teachers and other functionaries. This in-service teacher education helps teachers remain updated about new trends and practices in Elementary Education. The various strategies can be used to improve the training. Following are important strategies are as follows:

- Familiarisation training on new curriculum and textbooks
- Examination reforms
- Training of teachers on Inclusive Education for children with special needs
- Resource groups are strengthened at all levels (separate resource groups for each subjects) 300-350 Resource Person per district Follow up activities, on-site support and review meetings are

ensured. DIETs identified training needs – hard spots and develop training modules for teachers. This process helped to improve the quality of training.

- Training and retraining of teachers
- Planning and implementation of quality education measures
- Familiarisation training on National Curriculum Frame Work (NCF 2005)
- Scholastic and non-Scholastic areas improvement
- Training on grading system and assessment and the impact of grading system

(8) Distance education: Sponsored by Ministry of Human Resource Development, Government of India, the Distance Education Programme (DEP) is a national component of SSA. The responsibilities to implement DEP activities are entrusted to Indira Gandhi National Open University (IGNOU) in collaboration with all States/Union Territories of India. The DEP-SSA plays an important role in empowering teachers and other personnel associated with elementary education. It supplements the face-to-face training by using multi-media packages like self-learning materials, audio-video programmes, radio broadcast, teleconferencing, etc.

Q17. What is Mid-Day-Meal Scheme? Discuss.

Ans. Mid-Day Meal Scheme was introduced on a large scale, in 1960s in Tamilnadu, which was universalised in 1982 for all children up to class 10. Tamil Nadu's midday meal programme is among the best known in the country though the scheme is as good in Pondicherry. Several other states of India like Gujarat started it in late 1980s and Kerala started the same since 1995 and so did Madhya Pradesh and Orissa in small packets. The programme has become almost universal by 2005.

The success was so spectacular that in 1995, the Government of India began the 'National Programme For Nutrition Support to Primary Education'. According to the programme, the Government of India will provide grains free of cost and the states will provide the costs of other ingredients, salaries and infrastructure. Since most state governments were unwilling to commit budgetary resources, they just passed on the grains from Government of India to the parents. This system was called provision of 'dry rations'. On 28 November 2001, the Supreme Court of India gave a famous direction that made it mandatory for the State Governments to provide cooked meals instead of 'dry rations'. The direction was to be implemented from June 2002, but was violated by most states. But with sustained pressure from the court, media and in particular, from the 'right to food campaign', more and more states started providing cooked meals.

In May 2004, a new coalition government was formed in the Centre, which promised universal provision of cooked meals fully funded by it. This promise in its Common Minimum Programme was followed by enhanced financial support to the states for cooking and building sufficient infrastructure. Given this additional support, the scheme has expanded its reach to cover most children in primary schools in India. In 2005, it was expected to cover 130 million children.

Q18. Write a note on harmonisation of RTE Act, 2009 and Sarva Shiksha Abhiyan.

Ans. The Right of Children to Free and Compulsory Education (RTE) Act, 2009, which represents the consequential legislation envisaged under Article 21-A, means that every child has a right to full time elementary education of satisfactory and equitable quality in a formal school which satisfies certain essential norms and standards. From April 1, 2010, the right of children to free and compulsory education act has come into force. Every child in the age group 6-14 years will be provided 8 years of elementary education in an age appropriate classroom in the vicinity of his/her neighborhood.

Following are the objectives of harmonisation:

(1) To assess the awareness of regular school teachers, special teachers towards inclusion of children with special needs.

(2) To assess the attitude of regular school teachers, special teachers towards inclusion of children with special needs.

(3) To assess the possessed and required competencies of regular school teachers and special teachers to handle children with special needs in inclusive educational set up.

(4) To find out the significant difference if any, in the awareness of regular school teachers and special teachers towards children with special needs in inclusive education set up due to variation in their personal variables.

(5) To find out the significant difference if any, in the attitude of regular school teachers and special teachers towards children with special needs in inclusive education set up due to variation in their personal variables.

(6) To find out the significant difference if any, in the possessed and required competencies of regular school teachers and special teachers to handle children with special needs in inclusive education set up due to variation in their personal variables.

(7) To assess the attitude of normal students towards inclusion of children with special needs.

(8) To find out the significant difference if any, in the attitude of students towards children with special needs in inclusive education set up due to variation in their personal variables.

(9) To find out the relationship between the awareness, attitude, possessed and required competencies of regular school teachers and special teachers to handle children with special needs in inclusive education set up.

As per the norms prescribed under Sarva Shiksha Abhiyan, the right to free and compulsory education is guaranteed to children. According to the government norms, there should be a government primary school for a population of 300 at a distance of every one kilometre and an upper primary school for a population of 800 at every two kilometres. Seventh All India School Education Survey identified 10,30,996 recognized primary, upper primary, secondary and higher secondary schools in the country. These schools are further segregated over rural and urban areas. The rural area has 8,53,184 schools, whereas the urban area has 1,77,812 schools. Of these, the percentage of primary, upper primary, secondary and higher secondary schools is 63.15, 23.79, 8.80 and 4.26 respectively.

In Utter Pradesh, a number of children under the age of 6-14 are engaged in some form of work. If the records of the labour department are to be believed, over 5,000 children working in hazardous and non-hazardous industries have been identified and rescued so far since December 1996 in Varanasi, Chandauli, Jaunpur and Ghazipur districts. According to the additional Labour Commissioner D K Kanchan, 70 special schools for child labour under the National Child Labour Project (NCLP) are being run in Varanasi district while there are 30 such schools in Jaunpur and 20 in Ghazipur district. For three years, education is provided by each school to so children.

According to the All-India Educational Survey, there are 3,878 urban centers or localities in the country with an estimated population of 190.5 million. These have access to 74,656 schools, which have facilities for at least 4-5 years of education. This implies that there is one primary school for a population of about 2,500. Over 12 lakh Indian Children, aged between 5 and 14, continue to work in dangerous occupations like construction, and manufacturing industries all over India.

The RTE Act has implications for the overall approach and implementation strategies of SSA, and it is necessary to harmonize the SSA vision, strategies and norms with the RTE mandate. The MHRD set up a Committee in this context under the Chairpersonship of Shri Anil Bordia, former Education Secretary, Government of India, to suggest follow up action on SSA vis-a-vis the RTE Act. During initial meetings of the committee, it was conveyed on behalf of the Ministry of HRD that the committee may not strictly confine itself to the terms of reference and should as well make recommendations regarding implementation of RTE Act 2009.

Q19. Elucidate centralised versus decentralised system in elementary education.

Or

How can we achieve the goal of decentralised elementary education? [April-2016, Q.No.-27]

Or

Explain the role of decentralisation in the field of education. **[October-2016, Q.No.-27]**

Ans. The concepts of centralization and decentralization are important ones to consider as they ultimately affect the effectiveness of schools in educating the children of a nation. Centralization refers to the condition whereby the administrative authority for education is vested, not in the local community, but in a central body. This central body has complete power over all resources: money, information, people, technology. It decides the content of curriculum, controls the budget, is responsible for employment, the building of educational facilities, discipline policies, etc.

Decentralization, on the other hand, refers to the extent to which authority has been passed down to the individual school. Site-based management is an example of decentralization in which individual schools can make their own decisions related to finances and curriculum. However, the locus of power remains with the central body. Advocates of decentralization believe it will result in higher student performance; more efficient use of resources; increased skills and satisfaction for school administrators and teachers; and greater community and business involvement in and support for schools.

The process of decentralising primary education has already been initiated by several state governments. New legislations have been enacted by state governments to provide for the changed way of operating and creating a responsive system of delivery of primary education and framework for accountability. Some States have also gone for much closer collaboration and involvement of the community and the NGOs in delivering elementary education at the district level. On the whole, changing from a centralised to decentralise system has been a slow process. Towards the goal of decentralised elementary education, the country will continue to work by gradually shifting the focus of decision making from the State to the district, sub-district and community levels.

To ensure equity and inclusiveness of elementary education is the important objective of decentralisation. However, unless the reform is well planned and implemented, this objective may not be fully realised. As envisaged by the National Policy on Education 1986 and reiterated by several committees subsequently, the national government will continue to play a major role in coordination of institutional reforms and in monitoring the progress of reaching national goals of elementary education at the state level.

Some limitations are also there in decentralisation. Funding elementary education and shared distribution of power and responsibility may affect local accountability and efficiency. Each stakeholder puts the blame on the others for not achieving the objectives of UEE.

In elementary education, the idea of decentralised planning and management is a goal set by the National Policy on Education, 1986. The

Policy visualised direct community involvement in the form of Village Education Committees (VECs) for the management of elementary education. The Plan of Action (POA), 1992 emphasised micro planning as a process of tracking every child's educational progress regularly, and ensure that s/he continues his or her education at the place of her/his choice and completes at least eight years of schooling or its equivalent.

Q20. Briefly describe the experience of India with decentralisation.

Ans. Decentralization of educational governance has been a prominent element of educational discourse in recent years. In India, however, debates and policy initiatives related to decentralization emerged immediately after the country was liberated from British colonial control.

In India, a social system is stratified into manifold layers based on class, caste, gender, and religion. A good number of people belonging to marginalised sections do not have access to the basic amenities like housing, water, sanitation, electricity, health services and education. They struggle to make a living without basic education.

For the local self-government, the 73rd and 74th constitutional amendments have created a congenial ambience to play a more dynamic and proactive role. This shift has provided voice to women, Scheduled Castes and Tribes, minorities and others. In the context, others experiences will be reflected from the following:

- The National Literacy Mission also showed that when campaign mode was adopted to increase literacy levels at the district levels in which people participated actively, it had made a difference.
- The District Primary Education Programme (DPEP) launched in November, 1994 has also been so successful that the government has decided to adopt the DPEP strategy to operationalise UEE throughout the country.
- The ICDS experience showed that involvement of the local people is crucial to improve the health and nutritional status of vulnerable and disadvantaged children aged 0 to 6 years.

It is the main responsibility of DIET to plan the development of elementary education in the districts though the states continue to be ultimately responsible for coordinating and monitoring the progress of elementary education.

In planning and management strategy, the shift requires concerted effort to train and continually give support to educational professionals and administrators working at the urban local government and *panchayati raj* institution levels. Towards this end, in the education and allied sectors, the local level institutions are being strengthened in different states.

Due to the importance of Early Childhood Care and Education (ECCE), UEE aims to build on the base laid by ECCE (ICDS). ICDS depends on local community support to improve the pre-school children's health and nutritional status. ICDS is known internationally as one of the most successful programmes because of the involvement of the local community.

Following points are essential to obtain the active cooperation of the local community involvement:

- School Management Committees,
- Tribal Autonomous Development Councils
- Panchayati Raj Institutions,
- Parents-Teachers' Associations,
- Mother Teacher Associations,
- Village and Urban Ward/Slum level Education Committees,

Q21. Define and discuss planning and micro planning.

Or

What is meant by micro-planning? [April-2016, Q.No.-26]

Ans. Planning is proposing a set of actions or activities in a sequential order to achieve the required objectives or fulfill the needs. In other words planning is a process for indentifying the needs that exist in a particular area for achieving specific goals, evolving strategies to address them and proposing suitable activities as per the strategies.

Micro Planning: In its widest sense, educational micro planning covers all planning activities at the sub-national level, be it regional, local or institutional.

It is expected that the people living in the habitation take ownership and responsibility for making elementary education accessible to all children to ensure that the schools provide quality education to all children in a habitation. As teacher alone cannot play attention to needs of all the children, involvement of all the stakeholders such as women's groups, Village Education Committee members and members of *Panchayati Raj* institutions etc., is necessary. With the help of all the stakeholders ensure the all children, including disadvantaged group of society receive quality elementary education.

Q22. Enumerate and explain the steps for involving community in micro planning processes.

Ans. The steps for involving community in micro planning processes are given below:

(1) Empowerment of community

(i) For members of the Village Education Committee (VEC), School Management Committee (SMC), Mother Teacher Association (MTA), etc. conduct training workshops and build their capacity to identify issues concerning children's right to elementary education and find solutions

(ii) To make community aware of RTE provisions, their roles and responsibilities therein, conduct awareness campaigns and government efforts to universalise elementary education by undertaking activities, such as:

- Maa-beti Mela
- Kishori Mela
- Meena Campaign
- Prabhat pheris
- Mahile Sanmelan
- enrolment drive
- Bal, Shishu Mela
- cultural programmes/street plays at weekly community markets/fair focusing on specific issues to ensure increased enrolment and reduce drop out, getting certificates necessary for school admission, education of girl child, entitlements intended for disadvantaged special groups like the SC/ST/OBCs, nomadic/pastoral groups.

(2) Identification of planning teams: For planning, a government official or a head-teacher alone will not be able have all the necessary information. To be able to think of every angle of UEE a core planning team has to be formed. The community will feel a sense of ownership as major stakeholders are involved in setting the objectives and deciding the priorities. Legitimacy to the plan is come from involving a core planning.

We get the opportunities to identify individuals by interaction with community and target groups, these individuals can be members of ***core planning team*** for every habitation. Some may be educated; some may be politically active; some youth may be bubbling with ideas and enthusiasm; others may be willing to give their expertise; women may be resourceful; and minorities may have educated unemployed persons. Their involvement

(i) extend community support to prevent drop-out, migration, exclusion,

(ii) is educative in molding the opinions of the stakeholders in favour of inclusive education, and

(iii) contributes to building and strengthening of community-school linkages.

Core planning team's members selection has to be done carefully so as to include some who disagree with what is being done. Some may be vocal, dominating and imposing their ideas on others. There are some members in the team who may not measure up to the expectations but extend solid support to the teachers, the school and local authorities in making elementary education inclusive. It takes all kinds of people to deliver elementary education to all children. All sections of the community should be represented ideally by core planning team.

(3) Capacity building of core planning teams

Core planning team is important for the quality of the planning exercise and the plans. Proposed plans have to be 'do-able' at the district.

Entire planning process is participatory to make sure that all aspects of educational development are taken into account and to make sure that no one or a group is able to hijack the process of planning in their favour. And planning also requires knowledge about a variety of schemes administered by different departments and how to make use of these schemes in a way that they converge. Not many of the members of the ***core planning teams*** may have had the exposure and/or the required expertise to contribute to the planning process and the plans. The School Development Plans are consolidated by core planning team and it prepares the village education development plans. The core planning team has to present the school's needs effectively at the village, the village's needs at the Block, and the Block's needs at the District level respectively. Therefore, two to three rounds of orientation workshops have to be conducted to familiarise them with the aims, targets and norms of SSA programme, information to be collected for plan formulation and for monitoring implementation. About making use of expertise available with cluster/block/district level resource centres, they also have to be obtained.

(4) Identification of issues requiring intervention: Assessing the issues related to access, enrolment, retention and quality of elementary education to decide whether they can be addressed within the village, habitation, block or district. Some may:

(i) require policy changes
(ii) have to be addressed in a collaborative way
(iii) be administrative issues
(iv) require support from district and state level authorities
(v) require updating/upscaling of norms

There may be intense competition at this stage between schools, villages, blocks, and districts to portray the issues and challenges faced by their area as more urgent than others in order to access available resources. At the outset, it is pertinent to mention that a solid database and clear visioning are essential for prioritising the issues to be included in the Education Development Plan. Sometimes, intra-districts planning workshops can be arranged for sharing of experiences. This is a good way to identify the issues and learn about some of methods that have worked.

(5) Data requirement and sources of data: To achieve specific goals all plans are time bound with a clear mandate. As RTE clearly states that all children complete eight years of elementary education, it is essential to look at the data about:

(i) number of government, unaided/aided recognised/ unrecognised private schools,
(ii) children belonging to SC, ST, Nomadic Tribes, Most Backward Castes, Primitive Tribes,
(iii) child victims of mass violence/atrocities,
(iv) all the children (girls and boys) up to the age of 14 years – enrolled, never enrolled, out-of-school,
(v) children of displaced families,

(vi) informal schools run by NGOs,
(vii) other disadvantaged children,
(viii) working children,
(ix) children living on streets/public places,
(x) children living in protective institutions,
(xi) children of prisoners/prostitutes,
(xii) children with disability, and
(xiii) children of migrant families.

It will be possible from the data to select the target group which can be brought into the school system.

The data should facilitate tracking each child's progress since planning is meant to focus on each child in the targeted age group.

In the preparation and regular updation of the Village Education Registers the VECs/SMCs also have a significant role.

The current situation is reflected by mere availability of data is not the only objective of data compilation. Data have to be used for diagnosis of the challenges, for identifying specific needs, for estimation of required resources, for planning interventions and for justifying demand for resources. Data based planning will ensure effective and optimal utilisation of available resources. Data also will be useful for sharply target. Though lot of data may be compiled, only pertinent data need to be used. Through the household survey, generated data forms the basis for habitation level planning.

Likewise, the household data thus collected is consolidated and compiled at the habitation level. A set of suggested proforma has also been designed to facilitate this activity. Once the habitation level data are consolidated, the same should be computerised and used for habitation level planning. The filled up household DCFs is stored as Village/Ward Education Register (VER/WER) which can be handy for the VEC members to monitor each child's enrolment and attendance in the school which then can be discussed in each VEC meeting.

(6) Micro-planning exercises: After the formation of core planning team, their capacity building has been undertaken, issues and intervention strategies have been agreed upon, and necessary data have been obtained, the micro-planning exercise commences. The exercise involves the following:

(i) deciding the activities to be taken up
(ii) fixing responsible official(s) and/or organisation to implement various activities
(iii) setting targets on enrolment, dropout, retention, passing rates of children and teacher-pupil ratios according to the category of children, locality specific objectives achievable within the time frame of one year
(iv) estimating time required
(v) sequencing the activities

(vi) preparing plan proposal

(vii) setting phases for achieving the targets

(viii) estimate each item of expenditure

Concisely, ***logical frame of action*** has to be prepared. ***Logical frame of action*** lists objectives, activities to be carried out for each objective, persons who will carry out the activity, time required, schedule of activities, budget head, allocation, and expected out come. Following are some of the vital aspects of teaching learning process within classrooms:

(i) Classroom organisation and management (seating arrangement, layout, organisation of teaching-learning groups, display of materials and usability),

(ii) Availability and use of teaching-learning materials and aids,

(iii) Facilities available for teaching learning within classrooms,

(iv) Teacher-Pupil Ratio,

(v) Strategy for involvement of the parents, taking help of local education friendly people, utilizing community resource persons for both scholastic and coscholastic areas of learning,

(vi) Classroom environment (including physical and social),

(vii) Children's participation in classroom activities (Verbal/non-verbal),

(viii) Teaching methodology and strategies adopted,

(ix) Scope for evolving and experimenting innovative, contextual pedagogy by the teachers.

All the activities of teaching-learning need not to take place only in the classroom. Sometimes it is more effective to take the children out on a nature-walk to teach a lesson on bio-diversity. Sometimes such activities will require budget provision. These will have to be built into the Educational Plan.

Schools generally conduct activities for holistic education and development of children's personality such as sports, yoga, cultural programmes, project work; activity based learning, exposure to life skills with regard to health, nutrition, vocations etc. Such a focus entails looking upon a school as a social institution that is the hub of community activities. Encouragement to gain work experience would require the attachment of children with professionals, farmers, artisans, in order to master the social and natural context. These activities need to be built into the teaching-learning process for the overall physical, social, emotional and mental development of the children. For playground, physical education/yoga teacher, play equipment, inter-school sports and other competition; these activities would require planning and budget.

Following the National Policy on Education in 1986 there have been several innovative schemes in elementary education such as Operation Blackboard, Teacher Education, Non Formal Education, Mahila

Samakhya, National Programme for Nutritional Support for Primary Education, and specially designed education projects by states like Bihar, Rajasthan, UP and Andhra Pradesh. Since TLM play a crucial role in all these innovative ideas and practises, it becomes necessary to assess the type, availability, suitability and usability of existing TLMs for implementing these innovative activities. For the purpose of purchasing and creating TLMs such as work books, teachers' guides, teaching-learning aids, educational kits, etc., there is provision of ₹500/- annually to every teacher. These can be included in the plan proposal.

To create a child friendly school environment, there should be the focus of the civil works. The school should be located in a land that is non- hazardous (low lying area, too close to highway, river or pond, underneath high tension electric lines etc.) and is easily accessible to all sections of children. The design of the school building should be functional and attractive. The interior of the classrooms should have adequate light and ventilation and space for storage, display and chalkboards. Barrier free features like ramp, handrails, etc. are to be made mandatory in each school to meet *Inclusive Education* requirements. Provisions for toilet and drinking water, electrification, boundary wall and playgrounds are essential in every school. There should be greenery around the school premises Existing infrastructure (rooms, toilets, drinking water, seating arrangements, storage spaces, computers and other teaching learning equipment to be installed, boundary wall etc.) that is usable, also that need minor/ major repairs and required new infrastructure should be correctly assessed and budgetary requirements should be included in the plan proposal. There is a conformity of the technicalities of construction, unit cost, system of fund flow, roles and responsibility of the community and the systems of account keeping with the 'community construction manual' if available. And budgetary provisions have to be made.

It is significant to know what provisions are available and how to show them in the plan proposal. Following points should contain in the draft plan proposal:

(i) objectives

(ii) Staff requirement

(iii) details on strategy for teacher training, textbook revision, development of modules/manuals

(iv) new work to be undertaken during the plan period

(v) monitoring, evaluation, social audit to be undertaken

(vi) Context/background/problem including demographic information

(vii) detailed plans for tracking progress of children

(viii) documents/reports to be published

(ix) Programme/activities

(x) Strategy

(xi) Infrastructure requirement

(xii) Statement of budget required for current year

(xiii) amount budgeted for each activity

(xiv) financial support from other sources

(xv) unspent amounts in terms of recurring grants which could lapse at the end of the financial year

(xvi) status of releases of central and state share of funds during the previous year

(xvii) unspent balance of grants on non-recurring items of expenditure which is to be carried over for current year from previous plan period

Activities' costing will have to be according to prescribed norms. The plan proposal should also contain relevant data on action taken reports, assessments aimed at understanding bottlenecks, policy and administrative clearances required/sought from the state authorities. Where any deviations from the norms are suggested in the plan, full justification has to be given. The process of plan formulation, minutes of plan meetings, workshops and seminars, etc. that the core planning teams have held with the stakeholders are to be clearly documented as planning is a statutory formal exercise required by RTE.

Every school – private aided/unaided, and government schools in a habitation individually prepare their development plan proposals in bottom-up approach.

Q23. Describe the role of DEO in monitoring the implementation of UEE.

Ans. The functions of planner, implementer, coordinator and monitor are combined by District Elementary Education Officer (DEO). S/he is to fulfill the following responsibilities in elementary education:

(1) Make sure availability of schooling facility both at primary and upper primary level in all the habitations

(2) For enrolling and retaining out-of-school children (migrant/street children, SC/ST/Nomadic Tribes children, children with special needs), take steps in school and to ensure that they are provided educational opportunities through establishment of seasonal hostels or other flexible (like the vasthi shala of Maharashtra government) and alternate schooling

(3) Creating an enabling environment for realising children's right to education

(4) To initiate campaigns for registering the birth of all children up to the age of 18 years in order to maintain records of all children

(5) Build capacity of different School Management Committees to monitor attendance of teachers, attendance of children, educational standards and availability of TLMs

(6) Set up Grievance Redressal Committees headed by the Chairperson of a PRI body or the Chairperson of the Education Committee of the concerned urban local self-government

(7) Involve PRIs in special intensive efforts required for enrolling and/or retaining all children

(8) Monitor teacher vacancies in schools and send reports about requirements to the higher educational authority

(9) Ensure access by providing residential facility to such children who live in areas where providing a school is not feasible

(10) Ensure that there are no end-of-year exams, no detention, no corporal punishment, and other forms of violations of child rights

(11) Ensure access by providing free transportation to and fro school to girl children and CSWN

(12) Ascertain physical and social access to education in the neighbourhood for all school-age children

(13) Monitor teacher vacancies in schools and send reports about requirements to the higher educational authority

(14) Ensure that the issues of gender and other forms of social exclusion are resolved in the social audit process

(15) Cooperate with District Officers of different departments to *ensure that* children belonging to the disadvantage groups such as children of SC/ST/Nomadic Tribes, OBCs, Muslim and other minority children, girls, urban deprived children, street children, child labourers, children of migrant/displaced families and children without adult protection etc *are not abused*

(16) Set up District Education Committee consisting of elected representatives, experts, activists, parents, headmasters and officials of different departments like the Women and Child Development Department, Health Department, Police Department etc in order to oversee the steps taken to ban screening of children before admission

(17) Ensure availability of Teaching Learning Materials, Equipment, child friendly and barrier free access to school environment.

Most significantly, DEO has to consolidate the plan proposals prepared by schools, villages, blocks and prepare District Plan. To arrive at a clear picture of current status of elementary education - availability of schools within walking distance to all children, spatial, social and school mapping has to be undertaken at least once three or four years.

Q24. What is school mapping? What steps are included in process of schools mapping? Discuss.

Or

What do you know about school mapping? Discuss its importance.

Ans. Primary education in India is predominantly funded and managed by the government. Therefore, investment decisions by the Government determine the pattern of expansion of education-al facilities. Over a period of time it is noticed that certain areas are more endowed with school facilities than other areas. School mapping is an essential planning tool to overcome possi-bilities of regional inequities arising from the investment policies of the public authorities.

School mapping incorporates spatial and demographic dimen-sions into the educational planning process. The major question answered by the school mapping exercise is where to locate educational facilities. Location of educational facilities depends on the norms and standards developed by the public authorities. Even within the norms and standards, many geographical areas may be eligible for opening of new schools. School mapping technique helps us to identify the most appropriate location of schools or their alternatives so that more number of children can be benefited from the same level of investment. The major objective of school mapping is to create equality of educational opportunities by leveling off of the existing disparities in the distribution of educational facilities. This technique is useful to plan all levels of education. However, it is more widely used for planning for facilities at the compulsory levels of education. School mapping is not confined to locating formal schools; location of alternatives to formal schools is a part of the school mapping exercise.

Thus, school mapping is helpful:

(1) to build a dynamic vision of the education services, including infrastructure, teachers, and equipment required so that all children, irrespective of their caste, religion, gender, or distance are provided education of reasonable quality

(2) to identify children who cannot access school for social, cultural, economic and/or logistic reasons

The following steps are included in the process of school mapping:

(1) environment building in the village,

(2) formation of a village education committee specifically for school mapping,

(3) training of members of the village committee to conduct school mapping,

(4) preparation of a rough spatial map of the village,

(5) conduct of a household survey,

(6) preparation of a final map indicating different households, the number of children in each household and their enrolment status,

(7) preparation of a village/school education register,

(8) presentation of the map and analysis to the people to get it validated and

(9) get people's suggestions.

Necessary support is extended by the District Resource Centre (DRC) for preparing school mapping. It may be noted that the plans are not merely statements of a number of interventions or arithmetic of budgetary figures required to achieve the goals of UEE. At the district level, the plans serve as guide for monitoring the progress of UEE.

Q25. What is appraisal of a plan? Who appraises the annual District Education Development Plan?

Ans. Before finalization of the district plan, it goes through a process called "appraisal". "Appraisal" involves finding out the following:

(1) if justification of needs is convincing,

(2) if proposed intervention strategies are do-able within the time frame,

(3) what the threats and opportunities are,

(4) if the data provided as evidence is based on real situation,

(5) if the proposal plans are financially, technically, socially and politically viable and feasible,

(6) if progress can be made by filling the gaps between the present status and the ultimate goal of UEE.

Upon getting positive "appraisal", the draft plans are subjected to intense scrutiny by state government education, finance, women and children's development departments. State government departments may approve parts of or entire district plans, or request clarifications or suggest rationalizing targets. After changes are incorporated and resubmitted, the district plan may be approved and allowed to be implemented. Apart from preparing District Annual plan and the Perspective plan based on school mapping, the DEO has to implement the plans in collaboration with private schools, NGOs and other stakeholders.

Q26. What is meant by Public-Private Partnership in the context of Indian Elementary Education?

Ans. Basic primary education is generally perceived as public sector's responsibility, which makes any shared involvement of public and private sector a highly sensitive issue. Transfer of user fees to private sector providers and the management of public education institutions by the private sector are areas that are perceived to be very sensitive in the pretext to claim that governments are abandoning its core task of providing public education. In this realm, Public Private Partnership is a model in Education that has gained popularity over the past few years in India. The model has come to benefit the state, the non-state sector and most importantly the children. State government and local self-government bodies partner with Non-Government Organisations (NGOs), corporate houses, and other nongovernment organisations to complement one another to make different support services required to deliver elementary education effectively.

As a wide policy, it has been decided by the government to promote partnership with NGOs at all levels. NGOs that have been engaged in social development work for many years and have been running day-care centres, mobile creches, balwadis, charvaha schools, primary and pre-primary schools that have tremendous creative potential are identified in the district and are enlisted as partners to reach out to out-of-school children. Making such partnership with NGOs work requires change in the way government has been functioning at the local level. By the following three ways, partnership with NGOs is conceived:

(1) through funding by identified National and State Resource Institutions;

(2) through direct funding by Central and State governments; and

(3) through funding by Village Education Committees for implementing community activities.

In the following areas, RTE conceives a vibrant partnership with NGOs:

(1) ***capacity building*** - developing effective teacher training programmes, capacity building in communities and in resource institutions for planning and implementation

(2) ***develop innovative pedagogy***

(3) ***work with CWSN***

(4) ***improve transparency*** of programme interventions and assessment of achievements

(5) ***increasing awareness***

(6) ***research***, evaluation, monitoring of UEE

(7) ***expressing gender concerns***

(8) ***mainstreaming out of school children***

(9) ***advocacy, accountability***

Q27. Discuss the role of Community and BEO in monitoring and supervision of schools.

Ans. Role of the community

Monitoring and supervision of schools and other educational facilities in the village/ward, are the major role of VECs/Ward Education Committees and the community. Community based monitoring and supervision of implementation of plans is important to ensure that:

(1) enrolment, retention of education of girl children and other disadvantaged groups

(2) local level teachers are recruited where authorised

(3) all children come to school regularly

(4) school infrastructure is properly used

(5) TLM in schools are available and used for classroom teaching

(6) children receive quality education

(7) alternative schooling centers are conducted and properly monitored

(8) school timing is decided in consultation with VEC and parents

(9) children receive their entitlements

(10) grants are utilised for the purpose for which given

Role of BEO

With the help of Assistant Education Officer, Block Education Officer (BEO) is expected to:

(1) look at the condition of school buildings, infrastructure and seating arrangement for students

(2) look at the records required to be maintained by teachers and head teachers in schools

(3) obtain demographic information, number of villages, *panchayats,* clusters habitations, SC, ST, OBC school boys and girls, children in and out of school, children with special needs etc.

(4) visit every school including unaided private schools in her/his jurisdiction each year

(5) NGOs and other institutions delivering services to school age children

(6) pay particular attention to availability and hygiene levels of potable drinking water, toilets, kitchen where mid-day meals are cooked

(7) give feedback to the DEO about the felt-needs and requirements

Q28. What are the issues related with governance in elementary education.

Ans. There are some basic governance issues in the decentralised scheme of things in UEE, and these issues must be addressed. A mechanism to ensure that students' right of entry into the school system is upheld must be established. The mechanism may be as simple as requiring each school to publish its admission policy and to file an annual report listing the pool of applicants and admissions. Sanctions, such as partial withholding of funds or accreditation may also be considered. If choice is allowed, the law must address the related equity issues. Questions to be addressed include how choice is publicised, how students are selected, and what happens to those students who do not get their choice. The system as a whole would need to ensure that all students are accepted to at least one school, under reasonably equitable conditions. When these issues are not sorted out, it may result in unequal educational opportunities and failure to meet the guarantees given in the Constitution.

Following are some of the important governance issues:

(1) How will central resources be allocated to the various local bodies?

(2) Who will oversee and audit the finances of local authorities?

(3) If the central government is to continue to fund the local entities responsible for primary education, what assurance will the local bodies have that the funding will be secured and will continue?

(4) If local bodies are to be responsible for securing their own funds to finance primary education, what sources can they tap?

(5) If local authorities are to be given the power to tax, is the tax base sufficient to yield enough revenues for this purpose?

(6) What freedom will local authorities be granted in the use of the funds?

Q29. Briefly explain about issues of teacher recruitment and management in Elementary Education.

Ans. Decentralised management of teacher cadres is encouraged by the RTE Act. Certification, hiring, retention, and promotion of teachers are potential sources of contention and are generally addressed by law. When we say that UEE requires large institutional reforms, we refer to these governance issues. A time consuming process in taking care of all these issues is installing a system.

As long as these states are consistent with the norms established by NCTE these are free to follow their norms. The local government may recruit and the community may have a say in the selection process. There should be no compromise on standards. The RTE Act makes it mandatory that state governments have to ensure that there are no single teacher schools. It is to be strictly followed that at least 50% of the teachers are women.

In payments of salaries to teachers there is an existence of a lot of diversity. The presence of the non-governmental private schools and NGO initiatives makes the issue more complicated. Rationalisation of existing teachers' pay scales may become an issue.

Q30. What are the responsibilities of School Management Committee?

Or

What are the different government departments with which the School Management Committee has to work to protect child rights?

Ans. The constitution of a School Management Committee (SMC) is an important provision of the Act. Bodies similar to SMCs have long been in operation in different parts of the country to improve the monitoring and management of schools. While all schools have to constitute SMCs, there are some notable exceptions. In addition to the schools exempted totally from the Act, private unaided schools do not have to constitute an SMC. In minority aided schools and government aided schools, SMCS are to perform advisory functions only.

As per Section-21 of Right of Children to Free and Compulsory Education Act, 2009 read with Rule-3 of Odisha Right of Children to Free and Compulsory Education Rules 2010, School Management Committee shall be constituted in every school other than an un-aided school.

(1) 75% of the strength of the SMC will have to be form amongst parents or guardians of children.
(2) 25% of the strength of the SMC will be from amongst the following persons:
(3) One third members from amongst the elected members of the local authority, to be decided by the local authority;
(4) One third members from amongst teachers from the school, to be decided by the teachers of the school;
(5) Remaining one third from amongst local educationists/children in the school, to be decided by the parents in the Committee.

Protection of Child Rights: Protection of child rights include right to:

(1) freedom of expression
(2) survival
(3) protection from abuse and exploitation
(4) basic minimum infrastructure like housing, toilets, drinking water, bright class rooms
(5) books, blackboard, science lab equipment, teachers
(6) dignity and respect
(7) recreation and leisure
(8) health and development
(9) quality education
(10) family
(11) entitlements like free uniform, books, mid-day meal
(12) culture and heritage
(13) equal opportunity in accessing education

Primary responsibility to protect children's rights rests with the teachers, head teachers and the School Management Committee under the RTE Act.

Preparation of School Development Plan by SMC

The School Management Committee shall prepare a School Development Plan at least three months before the end of the financial year in which it is first constituted under the Act. The School Development Plan shall be for a three year plan comprising three annual sub plans. The School Development Plan shall contain the following details:

(1) Estimates of class-wise enrolment for each year;
(2) Requirement, over the three year period, of the number of additional teachers, including Head Teachers, subject

teachers and part time teachers, separately for Classes I to V and classes VI to VIII, calculated, with reference to the norms specified in the Schedule;

(3) Physical requirement of additional infrastructure and equipments over the three year period, calculated, with reference to the norms and standards specified in the Schedule;

(4) Additional financial requirement over the three year period, year-wise, in respect of clauses (1) and(2) above, including additional requirement for providing special training facility specified in section 4, entitlements of children such as free text books and uniforms, and any other additional financial requirement for fulfilling the responsibilities of the school under the Act.

Role of SMC vis-à-vis Relevant Government Department

According to the RTE Act, it is mandatory that every child must be in school; this pre-supposes that child labour is eliminated.

In RTE Act, inclusive education demands that SMC maintains vibrant partnerships with the departments and organisations concerned with children belonging to SC, ST, and educationally backward sections to ensure entitlements are made available.

Handling with children disabilities, SMC needs to work with government departments to make sure that equal opportunity for children with special needs is addressed.

To accelerate poverty reduction programmes, SMC needs to work with Rural Development and Panchayati Raj Department of the government so that children are freed from domestic chores and wage earning responsibilities and are able to attend school. And ensure that the Panchayati Raj institutions get appropriately involved and discharge their functions under the RTE Act.

Protection from corporal punishment, abuse and harassment are also included in protection of child rights. There is need for the SMC to closely cooperate with the National/State Commission for Protection of Child Rights and the state Department of Women and Child Development to ensure that children are protected from abuse.

Q31. What are the norms, standards and conditions with a school make a self decoration before commencement of the Act 2009? Also discuss the conditions for "recognizing" a private aided school after the Right of Education Act was enacted

Or

Why should only trained/qualified teachers be appointed by a school?

Or

Why is a private unaided school required to admit disadvantaged children?

Ans. The school also has certain responsibilities under UEE as per the Right to Education Act 2009. Every school, other than a school established, owned or controlled by the state government or Local Authority, established before the commencement of this Act shall make a self declaration within a period of three months of the commencement of the Act, in Form No. 1 to the concerned District Education Officer regarding its compliance with the following norms, standards and conditions:

(1) The school is run by a society registered under the Societies Registration Act, 1860 (21 of 1860), or a public trust constituted under any law for the time being in force;

(2) The school is not run for profit to any individual, group or association of individuals or any other persons;

(3) The school conforms to the values enshrined in the Constitution;

(4) The school is open to inspection by any officer authorized by the State Government/ Local Authority;

(5) The school buildings or other structures or the grounds are used only for the purposes of education and skill development;

(6) The school shall furnish such reports and information as may be required by the State Government, Commissioner and Director School Education and District Educational Officer from time to time and comply with such instructions of the State Government/Local Authority as may be issued to secure the continued fulfillment of the conditions of recognition or the removal of deficiencies in working of the school;

(7) The school shall maintain norms and standards specified under section 19 of the Act;

(8) The school shall give reservation of minimum of 25% in class I for the children of disadvantaged groups and children of weaker sections from the neighbourhood area. In case the private school is an aided school it shall provide free and compulsory elementary education to such proportion of children admitted therein as its annual recurring aid or grants so received bears to its annual recurring expenses, subject to a minimum of 25%.;

(9) The school having pre-school education shall also give reservation of at least 25 % of its enrolment at the initial stage of admission to the children of disadvantaged groups and the children of weaker sections of the neighbourhood area under section 12 of the Act;

(10) The school shall submit, every year, before commencement of the academic session, fee to be charged from the children to the District Educational Officer;

(11) The school shall comply with the provisions of the Act;

(12) The recognition shall be withdrawn in case of violation of the conditions of recognition.

A government, aided and unaided private school has to admit children belonging to weaker sections and disadvantaged group under the Part IV Section 7 (1, 2, 3) of the Draft Model Rules, for the purposes of getting recognition. Failing to do so will invite warning and/or withdrawal of recognition. And, such children shall not be segregated from other children in the classrooms, nor shall their classes be held at places and timings different from the classes held for the other children. In any manner, they shall not be discriminated from the rest of the children pertaining to entitlements and facilities such as textbooks, uniforms, library and ICT facilities, extra-curricular and sports.

A prescribed by NCTE, NCERT and the SCERT, the school is required to appoint qualified trained teachers. Failing to appoint trained teachers may result in de-recognition of the school. Where a state does not have adequate institutions offering teacher education courses, or persons possessing minimum qualifications are not available in sufficient numbers in relation to the requirement of teachers estimated, the state government will have to request, within one year of the commencement of the RTE Act, the Government of India for relaxation of the prescribed minimum teacher qualification. The Government of India may relax the minimum qualifications by way of a Notification specifying the nature of relaxation and the time period, not exceeding three years, but not beyond five years from the commencement of the RTE Act, within which the teachers appointed under the relaxed conditions has to acquire the minimum qualifications prescribed by the academic authorities. A person appointed as a teacher within six months of the commencement of the RTE Act, must possess at least the academic qualifications not lower than higher secondary school certificate or equivalent. The management of such school in which teacher does not possess the minimum qualifications at the time of commencement of the RTE Act shall enable such teacher to acquire such minimum qualifications within a period of five years from the commencement of the Act.

Q32. What are the Information and Communication Technologies (ICTs) for management of UEE.

Ans. We are in a digital era. It is difficult to think of any event in our daily life that is not using Information and Communication Technology. Our schools and classrooms are no exceptions. ICT, or information and communications technology (or technologies), is the infrastructure and components that enable modern computing. The use of information and communications technologies (ICTs) is to communicate and create, store, manage, distribute and use information for effective delivery of UEE. It is especially important for *school Net* that users are able to communicate, collaborate and exchange information online. In this context, ICTs typically refer to computers, computer networks, Internet, telephones, television, radio and audio-visual equipment and increasingly other devices used as network or Internet access devices such as hand-held PDAs (Personal digital assistant are electronic devices) and mobile phones.

People can participate fully when they have easy and affordable access to ICTs and communication networks, while those without have fewer opportunities. And, it is often assumed that ICT infrastructure and equipment are available. The phenomenon of different access to ICT is often labeled the "digital divide".

Language (ability to use languages that is widely used on the Internet), *literacy* (specifically a culture of reading) and *learning* (level of educational attainment)—these are three drivers of ICT usage. Education is one of the most important components in creating knowledge societies, economic growth and prosperity. Education is not only the means by which individuals become skilled participants in society and economy it is also one of the key drivers in expanding ICT usage. An environment will be built by the development of ICT in which most knowledge/information is shared; and more knowledge is created as the distribution of such information increases.

In the context of the transition to more inclusive UEE and decentralised education system, it is necessary to address structural problems and deficits in education systems. Using ICTs to enhance administrative and teaching efficiency to alleviate under-resourcing in specific areas (e.g., a lack of textbooks or teachers and other support materials), to address equity issues, or to support teachers who may be under-equipped to deal with new teaching challenges.

Q33. What is a School NET? Enumerate its functions.

Ans. The term 'School Net' is a shortened version of 'school networking'. School networking is the electronic connection of schools and students for purposes of enhancing teaching and learning. The physical facility and organisational entity that builds and maintains this connection is what is referred to as a School Net.

Organisationally, School Nets exists in a wide variety of forms. A School Net could be a programme located within a government department, a non-government organisation (NGO), a private company, or a school. It enables all the stakeholders access information about UEE located anywhere in the world. We can understand School Net as national/state level programme that is aimed at developing and supporting the use of ICTs in schools.

Disparate educational institutions are integrated by School Nets and they lay the foundation for management of education information system, and database for delivery of effective educational services.

Functions of School NET: Following are some of functions, activities and services provided by School Nets:

Technology services

(1) Supplying appropriate equipment to schools (purchased through government funding, sponsored through donor or corporate funding, or donations)

(2) For schools, government authorities, general public, connectivity services act as an Internet Service Provider (ISP), and facilitate partnerships between different organisations/systems

(3) Developing appropriate software solutions for management of delivery of education in schools

Content services

(1) Locally developed online content

(2) Content development at a professional level (developed by content specialists) or grassroots level (contributed by practicing educators)

(3) Portal sites to direct administrators, teachers and learners to appropriate Internet content (ideally organised and searchable)

Collaborative projects

(1) Designing and running collaborative projects on a country level, either original projects or localised international projects

(2) Facilitating involvement and collaboration of different resource centers in online projects

Professional development

(1) In-service training of teachers on ICT skills and using ICTs in teaching and learning (curriculum integration)

Experimentation, innovation and advocacy

(1) Developing and disseminating best-practice guidelines

(2) Conducting pilot projects across a range of environments and circumstances

(3) Advocating policy changes at various levels based on experience with pilot projects and best-practice knowledge

(4) Promoting and supporting innovation in the application of educational technologies

Management of school and resources

(1) Providing information support for policy making

(2) Providing information support for decision-making

Q34. Briefly explain School Net as Education Management Information Systems.

Ans. The efficiency and speed of data collection from schools can be substantially improved by ICTs and reduce the amount of effort spent on administrative functions. As a change management strategy, ICT tools and systems that are of direct value in reducing administrative work or providing greater access to information.

Everything will change in the environment after entering school net in school. ICT skills are seen as encompassing a range and types of skills, from basic applications competence, such as the ability to send an e-mail message, to higher-order skills such as the ability to locate, evaluate, analyse and synthesise information from a variety of sources (referred to as information literacy). These higher-order skills apply across all areas of management.

Q35. What is the pattern of sharing financing responsibility between the central and state governments in UEE?

Ans. The pattern of sharing financing responsibility between the central and state governments in UEE:

(1) The assistance under the programme of Sarva Shiksha Abhiyan will be on 85.15 sharing arrangement during the IX Plan, 75:25 sharing arrangement during the X Plan and 50:50 sharing thereafter between the Central Government and State Governments. Commitments regarding sharing of costs would be taken from State governments in writing.

(2) The State Governments will have to maintain their level of investment in elementary education. The contribution as State share for SSA will be over and above this investment.

(3) The Government of India would release funds to the State Governments/Union Territories only and installments (except first) would only be released after the previous installments of Central Government and State share has been transferred to the State Implementation Society.

(4) The support for teacher salary appointed under the SSA programme could be shared between the central government and the State government in a ratio of 85:15 during the IX Plan, 75:25 during the X Plan and 50:50 thereafter.

(5) All legal agreements regarding externally assisted projects will continue to apply unless specific modifications have been agreed to, in consultation with foreign funding agencies.

(6) Existing schemes of elementary education of the Department (except National Bal Bhawan and NCTE) will coverage after the IX Plan. The National Programme for Nutritional Support to Primary Education (Mid-day-Meal) would remain a distinct intervention with foodgrains and specified transportation costs being met by the Centre and the cost of cooked meals being met by the State Government.

(7) District Education Plans would inter-alia, clearly show the funds/resource available for various components under schemes like JRY, PMRY, Sunshchit Rozgar Yojana, Area fund of MPs/MLAs,, State Plan, foreign funding and resources generated in the NGO sector.

(8) All funds to be used for up-gradation, maintenance, repair of schools and Teaching Learning equipment and local management to be transferred to VECs/School Management

Committees/Gram Panchayat/or any other village/School level arrangement for decentralisation adopted by that particular State/UT. The village/school-based body may make a resolution regarding the best way of procurement.

(9) Other schemes like distribution of scholarships and uniforms will continue to be funded under the State Plan. They will not be funded under the SSA programme. The book you can most believe—GPH book.

Objective Type Questions

Q1. The right to free and compulsory education for children between age group of 6 to 14 has been inserted in Indian Constitution as–

(A) Article 46

(B) Article 16

(C) Article 45A

(D) Article 21A

Ans. (D) Article 21A

Q2. DIET stands for–

(A) District Institute of Educational Technology

(B) District Institute of Education and Training

(C) District Institute of Elementary Training

(D) District Institute of Elementary Teachers

Ans. (B) District Institute of Education and Training

Q3. The National flagship programme of education (SSA) aims at–

(A) Universalisation of Elementary Education

(B) Universalisation of Secondary Education

(C) Special Education in Primary Schools

(D) Special Secondary Academic Programs

Ans. (A) Universalisation of Elementary Education

Q4. The mid-day meal programme for Pr. Schools was initiated with a view to–

(A) Increase enrolment

(B) Involve community

(C) Engage teachers

(D) Increase the employment

Ans. (A) Increase enrolment

Q5. District Primary Education Programme (DPEP) was started in–

(A) 1990

(B) 1994

(C) 1998

(D) 1996

Ans. (B) 1994

Q6. _________ undertook the innovative project 'Lok Jumbish– People's movement for Education for All'?

(A) Bihar

(B) Madhya Pradesh

(C) Rajasthan

(D) Uttar Pradesh

Ans. (C) Rajasthan

Q7. Early childhood education for 3-6 years age group children scheme functions under–

(A) Sarva Sikhsha Abhyan

(B) Rajiv Gandhi Education Programme

(C) Universalisation of Elementary Education

(D) Sishu Vidya Yojana

Ans. (C) Universalisation of Elementary Education

Q8. The funds provided under 'Research and Evaluation' in SSA can be utilised for–

(A) government schools only

(B) aided schools only

(C) both government and aided schools

(D) un-aided schools only

Ans. (C) both government and aided schools

Q9. RTE conceives a vibrant partnership with NGOs in the area of –

(A) developing traditional pedagogy

(B) expressing moral concerns

(C) inculcating scientific attitude

(D) capacity building

Ans. (D) capacity building

Q10. The combination of primary and upper primary schooling is termed as –

(A) elementary education

(B) universalisation of education

(C) secondary education

(D) pre-basic education

Ans. (A) elementary education

Q11. The objective of the Lok Jumbish Project was to achieve education for all by the year

(A) 1995

(B) 2000

(C) 2010

(D) 2015

Ans. (B) 2000

Q12. RTE conceives a vibrant partnership with NGOs in the area of

(A) assessing the functioning of RTE

(B) conducting the programmes to improve discipline

(C) promoting the teachers

(D) expressing gender concerns

Ans. (D) expressing gender concerns

Q13. Bihar Education Project (BEP) was initiated in 1991-92 in

(A) 3 districts

(B) 4 districts

(C) 5 districts

(D) 6 districts

Ans. (A) 3 districts

Q14. Under SSA, funds will be transferred to VECs/SMCs/ Gram Panchayats for

(A) maintenance and repair of schools

(B) upgradation of schools

(C) salary of teachers

(D) Both (A) and (B)

Ans. (A) maintenance and repair of schools

Q15. Which one of the following is not a major component of DPEP?

(A) Civil Works

(B) Quality Improvement

(C) Management

(D) School Mapping and Micro Planning

Ans. (B) Quality Improvement

Q16. The government of Maharashtra has invented different projects. This/these is/are–

(A) Matru Probodhan

(B) Savitribai Phule parent adoption scheme

(C) Sakharshala

(D) All of the above

Ans. (D) All of the above

Q17. The Sarva Shiksha Abhiyan is to provide useful and relevant elementary education for all children in the –

(A) 5 to 10 age

(B) 7 to 12 age

(C) 6 to 14 age

(D) 10 to 18 age

Ans. (C) 6 to 14 age

Q18. Which of the following is essential to obtain the active cooperation of local community involvement?

(A) School Management Committees

(B) Planning Team

(C) Stakeholders

(D) NGOs

Ans. (A) School Management Committees

Q19. What are the vital aspects of teaching-learning process?

(A) Teaching methodology and strategies adopted

(B) Sequencing the activities

(C) Involvement of the teaching community in the planning process

(D) Effective teaching-learning activities

Ans. (A) Teaching methodology and strategies adopted

Q20. The SMC will have to prepare a School Development Plan at least ________ before the end of the financial year.

(A) Three months

(B) Four months

(C) Two months

(D) Five months

Ans. (A) Three months

Q21. Who sponsored DEP?

(A) HRD

(B) MHRD

(C) DPEP

(D) UEE

Ans. (B) MHRD

Feedback is the breakfast of Champions.

Ken Blanchard

You can Help other students.
"Inform any error or mistake in this book."

We and Universe
will reward you for Your Kind act.

Email at : feedback@gullybaba.com
or
WhatsApp on 9350849407

Elementary Education in India in the Cotemporary Context-II

INTRODUCTION

Universal elementary education has been at the centre of attention in discussions of both democracy and development. The gains from universal elementary education can hardly be overstated. It has important advantages for the individual and the nation. It expands the realm of choices available to the individual in almost every instance. The benefits in terms of key demographic variables such as infant mortality rate and fertility rate are substantial. Equally, it is important for the effective functioning of democratic institutions, the malfunctioning of which impinge on virtually every economic and social outcome. Elementary education covers the primary (6-11 years) and upper primary (11-14 years) age group. In most Indian states, this translates into the successful completion of prescribed educational requirements till Class VIII. If we compromise on quality and allow the mechanical expansion of poor schools for poor children, it should come as no surprise if the gains we had anticipated from universalising elementary education are not realised.

Q1. Identify the pedagogical issues and concerns of the primary and upper primary sub-stage of elementary education.

Or

Mention any two core components of quality in education.
[April-2016, Q.No.-28]

Or

What does quality in education include?

[October-2016, Q.No.-28]

Ans. From the inequalities of gender, caste, language, culture, religion or disabilities disadvantages arise in education. They need to be addressed directly, not only through policies and schemes but also through the design and selection of learning tasks and pedagogic practices, from early childhood, particularly at elementary education.

To include the rich inheritance of different cultures and the diversity UEE makes us aware of the need to broaden the scope of the curriculum. The development of self-esteem and ethics, and the need to cultivate children's creativity, are of primary importance.

In preparing teacher education programme at elementary level, the issues and concerns which need serious consideration and need to be addressed are as follow:

- **Curriculum design:** Curriculum must reflect the commitment to Universal Elementary Education (UEE), not only in representing cultural diversity, but also by ensuring that children from different social and economic backgrounds with variations in physical, psychological and intellectual characteristics are able to learn and achieve success at elementary level.
- **Systemic reforms:** In our country, the education system mainly encourages the individuals who memorise the textbook material and answer accordingly rather than the individuals who answer creatively. This approach lacks educational depth. Basically, it tests how much the student has mugged the given material. The society also encourages them who score the most, in examinations rather than the one who applies his learning in day to day activities. Various other factors which lead to all round development (personal, social, emotional) of an individual are barely taken into account in the grading scheme. It is precisely these factors that would determine the effectiveness of an individual in life. In student's career as well as life, education needs to focus on the values and principles that are at the core of the success.
- **Panchayati Raj Institutions:** To make the system less bureaucratic, teachers more accountable, and the schools more autonomous and responsive to the needs of children panchayati raj institutions offer many opportunities. Decentralisation and

emphasising the role of PRIs as systemic reform may accentuate local physical conditions, local life and local environment. Children acquire various skills naturally, while growing up in their environment. They also observe life and the world around them. When they bring their questions and queries to the teacher it will enrich the curriculum and make it more creative. Such reforms will also facilitate the practice of the widely acknowledged curricular principles of moving from "known to the unknown", from "concrete to abstract", and from "local to global".

- **Critical pedagogy:** In critical pedagogy, it is considered that how education can provide individuals with the tools to better themselves and strengthen democracy, to create a more egalitarian and just society, and thus to deploy education in a process of progressive social change. It is an educational movement, guided by passion and principle, to help students develop consciousness of freedom, recognise authoritarian tendencies, and connect knowledge to power and the ability to take constructive action. Critical pedagogy includes relationships between teaching and learning. This process takes place continuously in unlearning, learning and relearning, reflection and evaluation, and the impact of these actions on the students.
- **Curricular Concerns**

(i) Protection of environment: During the last century, the emergence of new technological choices and living styles has led to environmental degradation and vast gaps between the advantaged and the disadvantaged. It is our duty to nurture and preserve the environment. In the educational process, the need to create awareness of environmental concerns by integrating it at all stages of education and for all sections of society was one of the important core elements in NPE 1986. However making students sensitive to the environment and the need for its protection is still a major concern. Connect the learning in school to life outside the school is required by a conscious effort.

(ii) Peace Education: We live in an age of unprecedented violence; local, regional, national and global. In human relations, triggering intolerance and conflict, a disturbed natural and psycho-social environment often leads to stress. Sound development of an individual's personality can take place only in an ethos marked by peace. Education should empower individuals to choose peace as a way of life and enable them to become managers rather than passive spectators of conflict.

(iii) Democracy as a way of life: The Constitution of India guarantees that all citizens have right to justice, liberty and equality. Democracy requires as well as creates a kind of citizen who pursues one's own autonomy and respects others' right to do so. Education should function as an instrument of social transformation and an egalitarian social order; to inculcate among children respect for all people regardless of their religious beliefs. To strengthen our cultural heritage and national identity, the curriculum should enable the students to reinterpret and re-evaluate the past with reference to new priorities and emerging outlooks of a changing societal context. In the Constitution of India, education should create citizens conscious of the rights and duties, and committed to the principles embodied.

- **Pedagogical considerations**

(1) In the curriculum, a weightage of 80 percent have been received by the pedagogical component. The curriculum lays a great deal of emphasis on teaching through child-centred, activity-based and cooperative learning approaches. Another important objective of the curriculum is enriching the trainee's knowledge of the content of school subjects.

(2) A concern for quality of life in all its dimensions is included in quality in education. Protection of the environment, concern for peace, democratic citizenship and a predisposition towards social change are the core components of quality. The representation of knowledge in textbooks and other materials needs to be viewed from the larger perspective of the challenges facing humanity and the nation today. No subject in the school curriculum can stay aloof from these larger concerns, and, therefore, in terms of socio-economic and cultural conditions and goals, the selection of knowledge proposed to be included in each subject area requires careful examination.

There are some points of concern which requires planning and implementation:

- enriching the curriculum to provide for overall development of children rather than remaining textbook centric,
- nurturing an over-riding identity informed by caring concerns within the democratic polity of the country,
- making examinations more flexible and integrated into classroom life,
- using knowledge and skills of children from underprivileged sections of society to gain a definite edge and respect among their peers from privileged sections.
- connecting classroom knowledge to the experiences of children;
- ensuring that learning is shifted away from rote memorization,
- connecting knowledge to life outside the school.

Q2. Explain the main features of the NCF, 2005.

Ans. The NCF, 2005 document draws its policy basis from earlier government reports on education as Learning Without Burden and National Policy of Education 1986-1992 and focus group discussion. The approach and recommendations of NCF, 2005 are for the entire educational system. A number of its recommendations, for example, focus on rural schools. The syllabus and textbooks based on it are being used by all the CBSE schools, but NCF-based material is also being used in many State schools.

NCF, 2005 is divided into five areas:

- Perspective
- Learning and knowledge
- Curricular area, School stages and assessment
- School and Classroom Environment
- Systemic Reforms

The main features of the NCF 2005 are strengthening a National System of Education with special focus on-

- Values enshrined in the Constitution of India,
- Reduction of curriculum load,
- Ensuring quality of education for all (EFA)
- Systemic changes,
- Common school system

The NCF 2005 has recommended five guiding principles for curricular development

- Connecting knowledge to life outside school,
- Ensuring that learning shifts from rote methods,
- Enriching curriculum so that it goes beyond text books,
- Making examinations more flexible and integrating them with classroom life
- Nurturing an overriding identity informed by caring concerns with in the democratic polity of the country.

NCF 2005 also emphasises on learning and construction of knowledge:

- Correspondence between learner development and learning is intrinsic to curricular practices,
- Knowledge is different from information,
- Organising learning experiences for construction of knowledge and creativity,
- Connecting knowledge across disciplinary boundaries for insightful construction of knowledge,
- Learning experiences for developing critical perspectives on social issues,
- Plurality of textbooks and other material incorporating local knowledge mediated through constitutional values and principles.

It has also recommended significant changes in all five areas of language, mathematics, science, social science and Health Physical Education with a view to making education more relevant to the present and future needs. It has also recommended for softening of subject boundaries to enable children get a taste of integrated knowledge and the joy of understanding.

A teacher of the elementary school should be aware of the basic questions addressed in NCF, 2005 which are as follow:

- How can these educational experiences be meaningfully organised?
- What educational purposes should the schools seek to achieve?
- How do we ensure that these educational purposes are indeed being accomplished?
- What educational experiences can be provided that are likely to achieve these purposes?

Q3. Discuss the following:

(i) Pre-Service Training of Teachers

Ans. The regulations of the state education departments and examining bodies determine the professional skills of teachers in all categories of institutions except the unrecognised ones. The level of professional skill required is fixed in terms of academic and professional qualifications which are taken into consideration for granting recognition and affiliation. Therefore, institutions of various types, set up in the public and private sectors, adhere to the norms prescribed by the state.

Pre-service teacher training (initial training of teachers) is organised at the following three levels, i.e., pre-school teacher education, elementary teacher education, and secondary teacher education.

To train teachers mainly to teach primary classes from I to 5 elementary teacher education is organised. The minimum qualification for admission into the elementary teacher education program is either 10 or 12 years of schooling. Recently, most states have prescribed 12 years schooling as the minimum requirement though some states still have the entry qualification as secondary school examination. The program duration in the majority of states is two years, while in others it is one year. Elementary teacher training institutions are of three types-government, private aided and private unaided. Recently, DIETs have been set up in all the states. Providing pre-service and in-service education to teachers are important features of the DIETs.

(ii) In Service Training of Teachers

Ans. In context of NPE 1986, a national scheme of in-service training of teachers to reach out to elementary school teachers, was formulated by the Government of India. There are some of the programmes that are organized:

(1) **Programme of Mass Orientation of School Teachers (PMOST):** This programme is the example of in-service education activity. The main objectives of PMOST were to

sensitise teachers to the emerging concerns in education, UEE, use of learner-center approach, action research, the emerging role and responsibilities of teachers, enrichment of their knowledge in curricular areas, and other thrust areas enlisted in the NPE. This was a 10 days program in operation from 1986-90 covering about 1.8 million teachers implemented by the NCERT in collaboration with the SCERTs in different states. Films relating to various modules constituting the training print package were telecast on the national network for the benefit of teachers in different parts of the country. Each viewing session was preceded and followed by discussion. In the training, participatory, interactive approach was followed.

(2) **A Special Orientation Program for Primary School Teachers (SOPT):** To improve the quality of primary/elementary education as part of the strategy to achieve UEE, a Special Orientation Program for Primary School Teachers (SOPT) was launched from the year 1993-94. The main focus of this program was implementing the MLLs identified for the primary stage, training in the use of Operation Blackboard materials provided to primary-school teachers, supported by media and encouraging teachers to adopt a child-centered approach to teaching. Every year, it envisaged covering 0.45 million teachers.

(iii) Teacher Training for Special Needs

Ans. To look after children with special needs, the NPE 1986, recommended integrating children with locomotor and mild disabilities in general schools. The implementation of the UNICEF assisted 'Project Integrated Education of the Disabled' (PIED) in ten demonstration sites in different contexts further encouraged policy makers to integrate children with moderate disabilities in general schools, The Multi Site Action Research Project also promoted the need to develop 'effective' schools for all. All these experiences focus on the preparation of the general school system to meet the special needs of not only those with physical impairment but also of those with mental impairments and learning disabilities.

A provision has been made by the NCERT to orient all teachers and education officers by incorporating a component on special needs in all major in-service training programmes. The emphasis is on preparing general teachers and also moving towards the organisation of primary schools as inclusive schools focussing on meeting individual needs in the classroom. Teachers receiving this training are supported by multi-category trained teachers who were, provided training by 4 RIEs of the NCERT. Teachers absorbed into special schools, mostly single disability schools or those with multiple disabilities such as spastics, cerebral palsy, etc., are trained under the guidance of the National Institutes for the Handicapped as well as some non- governmental organisations with courses accredited by the Rehabilitation Council of India. In special education, a number of universities have also started offering B.Ed., and M.Ed. courses.

(iv) Curriculum for Teacher Education at Elementary Level

Ans. Specially, in the first three grades, the primary teacher is expected to teach mainly literacy, numeracy and life skills. Besides these, the teacher is required to have knowledge of the process of a child's growth, development and learning. At the secondary stage, with adolescent psychology and social processes, a teacher is expected to be familiar, in addition to knowledge of school subjects.

State governments/State Boards of Teacher Education develops the curriculum for primary teacher education and is reviewed from time to time. The curriculum for secondary teacher education developed by universities is also reviewed and updated periodically in the light of changes in the school curriculum, advances in pedagogical science, societal demands, technological advancements and changes in the socioeconomic structures in the country.

Model curricula for elementary and secondary teacher education have been developed by the NCERT. State governments and universities may adopt/ adapt this in their teacher education programmes. From time to time, the NCERT revises these curricula.

(v) Institutional Infrastructure for Training

Ans. For in-service training of teachers, the infrastructure exists at the central, state, regional, district and sub-district levels. At the national level, there are the NCERT, the NIEPA, the Central Institute of English and Foreign Languages (CIEFL), Hyderabad, and the Central Institute of Indian Languages (CIIL), Mysore.

At the regional level, there are Regional Institutes of Education located in the four regions of the country-Northern, Western, Eastern and Southern. One Regional Institute has been set up recently at Shillong for the states in the northeastern part of India.

At the state level, there are the SCERTs, State Institute of Education (SIE), State Institute of Science Education, IASE, CTEs, SIETs.

Districts have DIETs and In-service Training Institutes. DIETs cater to the in-service education of teachers working at primary and upper primary level. In-service education of secondary teachers is being looked after by CTEs. It is proposed to strengthen 200 CTEs, of which 73 have already been established. The IASEs are looking after the in-service education of senior secondary school teachers, including principals of these schools and the faculty of DIETs.

Recently, in-service training centres have been set up at sub-district level, i.e., block and cluster level. Under the DPEP, to begin with, these centres are being established in the districts covered.

(vi) Recruitment of Teachers

Ans. Different recruitment procedures are followed by different states. In some states, the recruitment is made on the basis of the candidates performance in a competitive examination, whereas, in some other states, recruitment is made on the basis of the academic and professional background of the candidate. The merit of each candidate is determined on the basis of his/her score in the examinations he/she has passed in addition to previous teaching experience, if any. In some other states, a combination of the two procedures, i.e., performance in a competitive examination and merit determined on the basis of academic credentials is adopted, In an oral examination held through interviewing the candidates, some weightage is given to the performance of candidates.

Q4. Explain salient aspects of NCFTE, 2009-10 with respect to elementary teachers.

Or

The qualitative improvement of the complete range of education depends upon revamping the Teacher Education. Discuss.

Ans. There are two stages of NCFTE as follows:

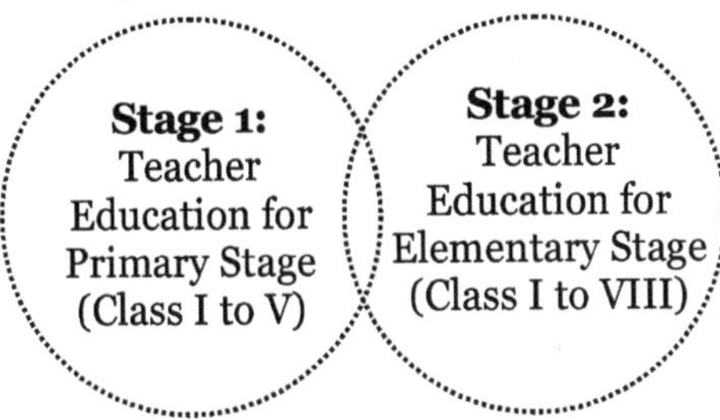

Fig. 3.1

Stage 1: Teacher Education for Primary Stage (Class I to V):

(1) Rationale: Through training inputs, the teacher needs to be empowered to gain greater insights into the complexities of the society and the historical perspective of the developmental process. The teacher profile is changing particularly from teaching to facilitator of learning, so NCFTE suggests a flexible framework for elementary education with ample scope for adaptation to local environment.

(2) Course Content

- The Courses on Psychology of Teaching and Learning, Health and Physical Education, Education of Children with Special Needs are for the necessary theoretical component for understanding the learner, community and the society, the internal and external forces impinging upon the school and the internal and external variables operating upon the learner.

- School Organisation and Pedagogical Analysis of primary school subjects are essential as they provide a sound base to function as a teacher.
- The course on Emerging Indian Society mentioned in NCFTE takes into account the thrusts identified in NCF 2005, rights of children, human rights education, values and their broad features, perspectives of educational, social, economic and political development in the country, significant landmarks in the process of development in various fields including science and technology, etc. with a purpose of making the teacher aware of the contextual realities in which s/he has to work.

(3) Training

- In teacher's profession, they need to tackle many problems. Action Research is included in the training to improve the way, through which the teachers address issues and solve their problems.
- In the training program, integration of the theory and practice establishes meaningful and interactive bonds between them.
- Correlation within the curricular areas of learning and external environment is established.

For making the course content relevant and region specific, the NCFTE proposes that the states can include additional areas.

(4) Transacting Curriculum

- **Theory:** Transactional strategies invariably need to emphasise interactive, participative and activity-oriented approach. The transaction of curriculum will have place to place intra and inter-content variations. The theoretical component of the curriculum can be transacted by lecture-discussion, self-component of the curriculum can be transacted by lecture-discussion, self-study approach, seminars, media supported teaching wherever possible, tutorials and through practical activities. It is expected that the intending teachers acquire, during the course of training, mastery of competencies and skills that are basic to the making of an effective, reflective and committed teacher.
- **Pedagogy:** Practice teaching remains to be a weak link of curriculum transaction. This point of view has been substantiated and re-inforced by field surveys conducted by NCTE at different places throughout the country. In this framework, pedagogical analysis of school teaching subjects has been thought of as an essential component of practice teaching. By way of pedagogical analysis, a student teacher becomes conversant with the objectives of teaching a unit, the entry behaviour of pupils, classroom management and evaluation strategies. With this background of having looked into the pedagogical aspects of school teaching subjects, the student

teacher is likely to become more effective and confident in the classroom. As a necessary part of the training of primary school teachers, knowledge of content is given due importance during the course of training. Mastery of subject matter, the insight gained through pedagogical analysis and the foundation courses when thoughtfully integrated and used for classroom instruction will lead to improving the quality of education.

- **Practicum:** For internalising the theoretical concepts, practical work is an essential component. It will have to be planned on each aspect of the theoretical inputs. In addition, practical activities centring around different school-experiences, work educational, school community interaction, action research projects and other educational activities directed towards development of the personality of students will also be undertaken by the intending teachers. It needs continuous planning, analysing, monitoring and evaluation throughout the duration of the course, which will necessitate the involvement of teacher educators more vigorously than it is at present.

(5) The Role of Teacher Educators: At this level, the role of teacher educators in curriculum transaction becomes challenging as they need continuous planning, analysing, monitoring and evaluating throughout the course. This makes necessary the involvement of teacher educators more vivaciously than now.

(6) Evaluation: To determine the achievement of the desired objectives is the main purpose of evaluation. Evaluation helps in determining the effectiveness of any programme in meeting the objectives. The evaluation system should take into account the intended outcomes of the training program, in relation to Theory, Practice Teaching and Practicum. Naturally, it should take place throughout each phase of the process (CCE) and not only as a last step, so evaluation of each of these aspects needs to be carefully planned. Hence, there is an increasingly felt need to introduce internal continuous and comprehensive evaluation system replacing external examinations. This has already been introduced as a part of the evaluation system along with external examination though as possible by many, total replacement of external system by CCE is not considered.

(7) Tools for Evaluation: Appropriate assessment tools depending upon the objectives of each of the aspects need to be selected or designed; such as:

- Performance such as practice teaching, participation in various activities measured through check-lists, rating scales, and observation schedules etc.,
- Oral examinations,
- Paper-pencil tests comprising objective-based questions-A balanced combination of essay type, short answer type and objective type questions.

Evaluation can be external, internal or a judicious combination of both and assigning grades instead of marks is a professionally sound step as it minimises categorisation of students on the basis of marks eliminating unhealthy competition among learners. Leading to a stress free learning environment, it also reduces social pressures.

Stage 2: Teacher Education for Elementary Stage (Class I to VII):

(1) Rationale: From the constitutional commitment of providing compulsory education till age 14 the Right to education Act has evolved. This age range covers a gradual transition from concrete operational stage of development to abstract reasoning process. This demands transition of the teaching and learning processes and a gradual change in teaching-learning strategies from one stage to another matching with the maturity of learners.

(2) Course Content

- The course on Health and Physical Education will enable the teachers to plan exercises for development of sound. These will also be helpful to deal with children with special needs.
- The course on counseling and guidance will enable the teachers to help children when they are confronted with any kind of problem.
- The course on Education Emerging Indian Society will enable the prospective teachers to understand the demands that society expects education to fulfill. At this stage, a course on 'Elementary Education in India-status, problems and issues' is proposed which will promote the capacity to examine if these expectations can really be met.
- The course on Psychology of Teaching and Learning will enable the teachers to learn how to formulate their teaching strategies to promote learning among their students.

(3) Training: In the pre-instructional, instructional and post-instructional phases of teaching, the prospective teachers are to be prepared as to enable them to perform successfully. For this, the following capacities/abilities need to be developed:

- Internship in a school will offer varied experiences needed for working in a school. They will internalise educational value of the work and experience the dignity of manual work.
- At the elementary level, the pedagogical analysis will provide an understanding of the complexity involved in the teaching of the subjects. This will enable the teachers to plan the educational strategies. A critical observation of model lessons and practice teaching in the actual clas room situation will result in preparing an effective and competent teacher.
- The school community interaction would not only promote the interactive support between both but also enable to evolve suitable pedagogy for students. The organisation of education

activities will develop the capacity for planning and undertaking such activities as are essential for the development of personality of the student. To prepare a competent elementary school teacher, the theoretical and practical courses suggested in this frame are capable.

- Action Research will develop their capacity of problem solving.

(4) Transacting Curriculum

- **Theory:** Several well-designed approaches are needed to be adopted like lecture-discussion, cooperative study, practical and demonstration techniques, self-study as well as projects. The teachers should combine different strategies and instructional materials, use supportive media, plan more of hands on experiences, organize field trips and visits, etc. Due attention is to be given to children with special needs. According to the needs of students and locally available resources, the curriculum transaction will have to be adjusted.

- **Pedagogy:** The existing transactional strategies marginally promote the capacity for independent study, self-discovery and self-study during the process of teaching and learning. They rarely seek prospective teachers' participation and remain mostly a one way communication. The cooperative learning approach is taught through lecture, hence they are not able to practice the learner centred approaches. The above strategies will help the prospective teacher to practice them for their own students because they get a first hand demonstration of their use.

  Practice teaching is the weakest link of teacher education, possesses the potentiality of converting itself into a strong component if properly organised. The process of curriculum transaction needs improvement and enrichment. Pedagogical analysis of teaching subjects is sure to refine teaching and learning as it will transform the teachers' performance and develop competencies not covered by the method-cum-content approach. With the background of pedagogical analysis and model and demonstration lessons given by the teacher educator, the class room performance is sure to improve if it is supervised in detail by the subject specialist.

- **Practicum:** An important component of practical work is work education and its potentiality has to be utilised by teacher education for developing certain qualities of character. To evolve suitable teaching strategies, the mutually supported school and community interaction helps the teachers.

  To organise educational activities in school the teachers will be required. They have to learn to plan and organise such activities as are essential to provide opportunities for self-expression and lead to development of personality of students. They have to be trained for utilising supplementary materials essential for promoting and accelerating learning among students.

(5) The Role of Teacher Educators: The teacher educators will be facilitating physical, social, emotional and aesthetic development of the prospective teachers. Their creative and constructive potentialities need to be fostered. Practical activities will help to achieve these aims. It is, therefore, necessary to organize these activities on continuing basis. The influence of teachers' personality and behaviour has lasting impact on students. In the selection and adoption of transactional strategies, the teacher educator has to ensure that teaching becomes participatory, cooperative, activity-centred and joyful so that the prospective teachers can also bring about similar modifications in their teaching-learning practices.

To deal with specific situations, teacher education has to inculcate professional commitment, develop competencies and make teacher reflective.

(6) Evaluation: At this stage, to bring improvement in teaching learning process, evaluation has to be continuous, formative and comprehensive. In the curriculum process, systematic evaluation will enable a teacher to select proper teaching strategies and effect suitable changes.

At the elementary stage, the evaluation of the pupil teachers will not differ much from that of primary stage and the same principles and similar practices which have been adopted at the primary level may be utilised at this stage.

(7) Tools for Evaluation: Evaluation ascertains the success or failure of the curriculum transaction done by means of valid and reliable tools.

Q5. Write note on the following:

(i) 'Diploma in Elementary Education (D.El.Ed.)'.

Ans. Diploma in Elementary Education (D.El.Ed) programme is a specifically designed package for in-service untrained teachers working in primary/upper primary schools of different states of the country and having completed twelve years of school. The Programme aims at enabling the target group to develop in them skills, competencies, attitudes and understanding to make teaching and learning more effective. The curriculum comprises of three components:

(1) **Theory:** For D.El.Ed., first year comprising of nine papers and eight papers for D.El.Ed. second year including related practical work for each paper.

(2) **Practical:** This includes activities such as Microteaching, Practice Teaching, Social Service, Music, Arts and Physical education.

(3) **Internship:** It is useful to enhance the various teaching skills and practicing appropriate methods of six month duration.

(ii) Upgrading Elementary Teacher Education

Ans. Education is not merely an application of a few core disciplines it is an area of inter disciplinary knowledge, but a praxis and a context where theories and practical wisdom are generated continuously. The secondary teacher education institutions developed in due course into university departments of education and thus elementary teacher education and with their own distinct concerns, concepts and methodological perspectives early childhood education remained neglected as distinct areas of knowledge.

According to NCF 2005, the contents for a primary school teacher, of Pre-service training, must emerge from the roles and functions of primary school teacher and should have the potential to prepare the trainees to handle effectively the curriculum of primary classes.

In school system, D.El.Ed course is undergoing lots of changes, keeping in tune with the changing times and evolving perception about its role and significance. This is particularly relevant with the current initiatives like NCF 2005, RTE-2009, Human Rights and Child Rights, Fundamental Duties, Multiple Intelligence, Participatory Learning and so on. Incorporating the new themes which are well suited with the current scenario necessitates participatory curriculum planning involving all stakeholders. Some approaches are called for in teacher education processes modular approach, skill learning and practice, a professional approach to training strategies and development of materials, and application of relevant technological, curricular and organisational alternatives.

Keeping in view the role of the elementary teacher, the curriculum comprises different types of course contents, which may be categorised as under:

(i) Foundation course

(ii) Content-cum-methodology in different subjects

(iii) School Experience programme

(iv) Practical work

Education is closely linked with disciplines. In fact, its basic concepts have roots in other disciplines like Philosophy, Psychology and Sociology. To understand different processes of education, understanding of these disciplines, specially their implementations in education is of vital importance. To enable the prospective teachers, to develop insight into priorities and problems of teaching-learning processes are the major functions of these courses. It is presumed that concepts incorporated in these courses will equip the trainees to organise teaching learning processes in the classrooms in right perspective.

Q6. What is the need for new models in elementary teacher education? Discuss.

Ans. Initial primary teacher education has a special significance, since elementary education became a fundamental human right. Many of the students may leave the education system afterwards for various reasons but they have to contribute to the national development as productive and conscientious citizens and therefore to individual as well as national development it has a crucial significance.

To teach at the elementary level, the +2 entry level does not even equip prospective teachers with the basic knowledge of subjects, particularly classes 3 to 8. Neither does the short duration of the course equip them with the necessary pedagogic knowledge for facilitating the learning of children, understanding their psycho-social and learning needs.

Too general guidelines are provided by the earlier curriculum frameworks and also do not address the stage-specific training needs of elementary teachers. The Curriculum Framework (1998) was indeed a welcome exception. It may be the first to have provided stage–specific guidelines. In bringing the issue of elementary teacher education to the national stage, the establishment of DIETs has been the most important development.

In elementary education, the need for specially qualified teacher educators is not recognised till recently. It has been taken for granted that the existing arrangements for teacher preparation at different stages would do as well for teacher educators too, B. Ed. for elementary teacher educator and M.Ed. for secondary teacher educator. At present, elementary teacher educators upgrade their professional qualifications by pursuing M.Ed. The M.Ed. faculty also does the training of elementary teacher educators. In most of the states the present M. Ed. cannot meet the requirements of elementary teacher training as it is based on only secondary education requirements. Other than the activity of teaching children in elementary school, due to lack of appropriately trained personnel in elementary education, all other functions are performed by people who are trained for secondary level.

There is a grave need to upgrade initial teacher education by enhancing the entry qualification and duration of training.

Q7. What initiatives have been taken to improve the models of elementary teacher education?

Ans. Following initiatives have been taken to improve the models of elementary teacher education:

(1) **Innovative Courses to suit to Changing Needs:** According to many educationists, the initial teacher education programme should be made equivalent to a degree programme and there is a need to allocate the management and control of elementary teacher education to a professional body of university faculty status:

(i) TISS is conducting M.Ed. program in Elementary Education at Mumbai.

(ii) Jamia Millia Islamia have also started a few innovative courses; particularly M.Ed. in Elementary Education.

(2) **One Year B.Ed. Courses for Elementary School Teaching for Graduates:** To encourage upgrading of elementary school teacher training to higher education level, a one year B.Ed. (Elementary) course can be made equivalent to two year Diploma course for elementary school teaching.

(3) **The Bachelor of Elementary Education (B. El. Ed.) program of the University of Delhi - a 4 year integrated professional degree programme:** The Bachelor of Elementary Education (B.El.Ed) Programme is a four-year integrated professional degree programme of Elementary Teacher Education offered after the senior secondary level (class XII or equivalent). This is a bilingual programme, conceptualized by the Maulana Azad Centre for Elementary and Social Education (MACESE) of the Faculty of Education, University of Delhi. Launched in the academic year 1994-95, the programme is an attempt towards fulfilling the need for professionally qualified elementary school teachers. The B.El.Ed. Programme is designed to integrate the study of different disciplines to build a comprehensive understanding about education. The programme offers compulsory and optional theory courses, compulsory practicum courses and an intense school internship programme.

The B.El.Ed. programme aims to produce graduates of high caliber in the field of teacher education. A lot of effort is spent in the training of students and giving them a supportive and stimulating environment.

Some of the professional and academic opportunities available for B.El.Ed. graduates are:

(i) Teaching in elementary schools (Classes I to VIII): B.El.Ed. graduates are eligible for recruitment as teachers in MCD/ NDMC/Sarvodaya Vidyalayas in Delhi as well as in Kendriya Vidyalayas and Navodaya Vidyalayas across India, and in private schools.

(ii) Leading the elementary school systems in various capacities.

(iii) Teaching and research in elementary education in government and nongovernment sectors.

(iv) Post-graduate and research studies in education and allied disciplines.

(v) Serving as teacher-educators in various State Institutes and University Departments/Colleges offering pre-service education in elementary and secondary education.

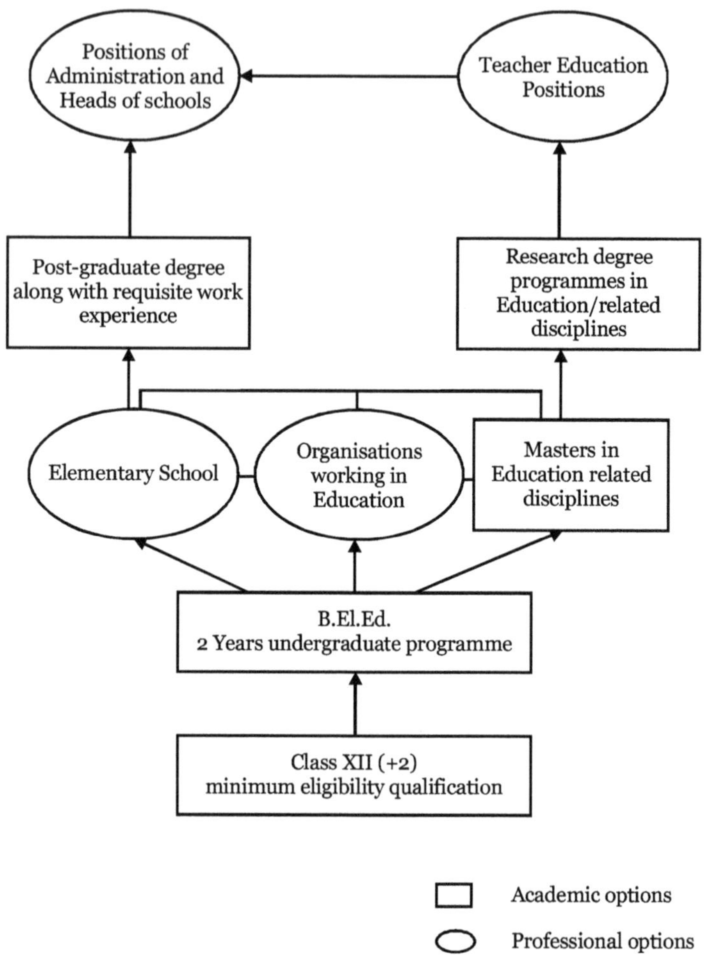

Fig. 3.2

(4) **Bridge courses to switch over from one stage to another:** The government of Uttar Pradesh is proving a programme to make B.Ed. passed candidates eligible for primary school teaching job through their participation in special BTC programme of 6 month duration.

Within a definite time frame a transition to the new models will need to be completed–say five years–keeping in mind the time required for preparation of teacher educators as well. However, after twelve years of schooling the present two year D.ED. model may continue making it as meaningful and relevant as possible.

Q8. What is reflective practice? Also discuss the origin of reflective practice.

Ans. In simple terms, reflection is a form of conscious response to a situation or event, and the experiences within that situation or event. "Reflection is a generic term for those intellectual and affective activities in which individuals engage to explore their experiences in order to lead to new understandings and appreciations. It may take place in isolation or in association with others. It can be done well or badly, successfully or unsuccessfully" Boud and Walker (1985).

According to Brookfield (1995) and Thiel (1999), "In reflective practice, practitioners engage in a continuous cycle of self-observation and self-evaluation in order to understand their own actions and the reactions they prompt in themselves and in learners".

Reflective Practice refers to taking action to improve on what one has learned. It is linking objectively thought and action to make changes. It involves thinking about and critically analyzing one's actions with the goal of improving one's professional practice.

A person learns from the experiences by critically reviewing the actions, considering the impact of those actions and planning what s/he would do in similar situations in the future is called reflective practitioner.

Origin of Reflective Practice: Most scholars point to John Dewey as the first educational theorist who suggested that teachers can improve their practices through reflection. According to Dewey (1933, p. 118), "active, persistent, and careful consideration of any belief or supposed form of knowledge in the light of the grounds that support it and the further conclusions to which it tends."

A person find himself, in every case of reflective activity, confronted with a given, present situation from which he has to arrive at, or conclude to, something that is not present. This process of arriving at an idea of what is absent on the basis of what is at hand is inference.

Dewey viewed reflection as a holistic approach to teaching and a way for teachers to solve problems that occur in the classroom. He advocated three key components of the reflective process, which are as follows:

(i) Open mindedness: Open-mindedness relates to a willingness to consider more than one side of an argument and attend to alternative possibilities. This requires an active desire to both listen and accept the strengths and limitations of your own and other people's viewpoints. In some instances, this may lead to the recognition that your former beliefs were misconceived. You may find that you made judgements about an issue and 'jumped to conclusions' without listening to others.

(ii) Responsibility: Responsibility relates to the disposition to carefully consider the consequences of your actions and to accept those consequences. When individuals profess certain beliefs (yet) are unwilling to commit themselves to the consequences that flow from them confusion and misconceptions often arise. By reflecting on your practice and questioning whether your actions were appropriate and effective in a given context, you will demonstrate responsibility within your work.

(iii) **Whole-heartedness:** Whole-heartedness relates to the way in which the attitudes of open-mindedness and responsibility are brought together through your interest and enthusiasm. Wholehearted practitioners are dedicated, and regularly examine their beliefs and assumptions along with the consequences of their actions. In this way, they adopt an approach to their work that is open and receptive to learning something new. The following activity provides a series of questions for you to engage with so as to better understand what is involved in the process of reflecting on your experience.

Q9. Write short notes on the following:
(i) Reflection: Experience with Feelings

Ans. The great strength of the work of Boud, Keogh and Walker (1985) is that they address emotions. For them reflection is an activity in which people 'recapture their experience, think about it, mull it over and evaluate it' (ibid: 19). They rework Dewey's five aspects into three.

(1) **Returning to experience** – that is to say recalling or detailing salient events.

(2) **Attending to (or connecting with) feelings** – this has two aspects: using helpful feelings and removing or containing obstructive ones.

(3) **Evaluating experience** – this involves re-examining experience in the light of one's intent and existing knowledge etc. It also involves integrating this new knowledge into one's conceptual framework.

(ii) Methods of Reflection

Ans. One would like to record a particular even or incident because he think it is critical or significant for him. He should record the situation, his role, result of his action and a reflection on the situation or event. It can be recorded in following manner:

(1) **A Narrative:** A story of an experience or event written in the first person is called a narrative. It enables links to be made between personal and professional development.

(2) **A Reflective Journal:** It is a reaction to the event or experience looked upon in different ways linking the experience with other experiences and the learning from the

situation. It also has record of what teachers need to learn and how they might achieve their identified learning goals.

Q10. Discuss the modern concept of reflective practice.

Ans. Building on the foundation laid by Dewey's early work, Donald Schon helped define the modern concept of reflective practice in teaching. He introduced the term 'Knowledge-in-action' which refers to the kind of knowledge that is revealed in the way we carry out tasks and approach problems. This knowing is in the action. This tacit knowledge is derived from research and also from our own reflections and experience. This professional knowledge increases with each reflective teaching experience, and allows teachers to continually take action based on this knowledge. He suggested that the capacity to reflect on action so as to engage in a process of continuous learning was one of the defining characteristics of professional practice.

He defined the reflective process as consisting of "reflection-in-action", "reflection-on action" and "reflection-for-action."

- **"Reflection-in-action"** refers to the reflection that happens while the action occurs.
- **"Reflection-on-action"** encompasses reflecting upon the experience before it begins and after it is finished.
- **"Reflection-for-action"** happens when knowledge gained from reflection influences future action.

Q11. Explain the key features of a teacher as reflective practitioner. Also discuss the traditions of reflective practice.

Or

Discuss the main features of reflective teaching trading highlighted by Zeichner and Liston (1996).

Ans. According to Zeichner and Liston (1996:6) model of reflective teaching, there are following key features of a teacher as reflective practitioner:

(1) takes part in curriculum development.

(2) takes responsibility for his/her own professional development.

(3) examines, frames, and attempts to solve the dilemmas of classroom practice,

(4) is attentive to the institutional and cultural context in which s/he teaches,

(5) is aware of the questions, assumptions and values s/he brings to teaching,

Five different traditions of reflective teaching are identified and detailed by authors Kenneth M. Zeichner and Daniel P. Liston in *Reflective Teaching: an Introduction*. These are:

(1) **Developmentalist tradition:** Developmentalist tradition means reflecting on one's approach based on students' backgrounds, interests, thinking and developmental and academic level.

(2) **Social reconstructionist tradition:** It stresses upon reflection about the social and political context of schooling and the assessment of classroom actions to enhance equality, justice, and more humane conditions in schools and society. Teachers need to be aware of the cultural, political and institutional influences present in their work and in the lives of their students.

(3) **Generic tradition:** The generic tradition represents the general reflecting teachers do in their work. The focus is on the belief that teachers should use purposeful reasoning for their actions.

(4) **Academic tradition:** The academic tradition focuses on reflecting on course content and how it is taught. Teachers must thoroughly understand the subject matter and develop dynamic activities that accurately convey material to students.

(5) **Social efficiency tradition:** The social efficiency tradition refers to using methodology rooted in scientific research as the basis for instruction and the standard by which teachers reflect upon their work. Teachers need to learn and implement the findings of research that show a positive correlation between specific teaching strategies and students outcomes.

The authors point out that each of the above traditions has been used separately for various teaching reform efforts and in teacher education. In practice, however, the majority of teachers use a combination of these traditions.

They also emphasised that:

- Good reflective teaching also needed to be democratic in the sense that teachers must be committed to teaching all of the students to the same high academic standards,
- If teachers did not question the goals, values, and assumptions that guided their work and did not examine the context in which they taught, then they were not engaged in good reflective teaching,
- It must be democratic and self-critical, and
- About the ends, means and contexts of teaching, reflective teaching entailed critical questions.

Q12. Explain about the education of scheduled caste children.

Or

What are the problems, which SC students are facing?

Ans. SC children remained aloof from the education system because these groups doing menial jobs. After independence untouchability has been abolished by law. However, a schedule of castes was prepared to ensure that these groups of people are given extra benefits to compensate for their deprivation. People belonging to Scheduled Castes (SC) are also guaranteed certain constitutional rights. Not only are they given free school education but are also offered a reservation in institutions of higher learning. These measures have increased the percentage of SC students in schools and colleges. Many of them have successfully completed higher education too. The literacy levels of people from these communities have seen a constant growth over the past sixty years. Nevertheless, thorough investigation and action plan the problem needs to overcome it fully.

The SSA Framework for Implementation has given the broad listing of examples of exclusion of SC children as follows:

(1) **Exclusion by Teachers**, in terms of segregated seating arrangements; undue harshness in reprimanding SC children; not giving time and attention to SC children in the classroom, including to answer their questions; excluding SC children from public functions in the school; making derogatory remarks about SC children and their academic abilities; denying SC children the use of school facilities; asking SC children to do menial tasks in school.

(2) **Exclusion by peer group**, in terms of calling SC children by caste names; not including SC children in games and play activities; not sitting with SC children in the classrooms.

(3) **Exclusion by the system**, in terms of incentives schemes meant for SC children not being implemented in full; a lack of acknowledgement of SC role models in the curriculum or by teachers; reinforcing caste characteristics in syllabi and textbooks; lack of sensitisation of teachers in teacher education and training; insufficient recruitment of SC teachers.

The interventions for children belonging to Scheduled Caste communities have to be based on the intensive micro-planning addressing the needs of every child. The following suggested list of interventions for inclusion of SC children can help in addressing the fore stated practices of discrimination and exclusion:

(1) Establishing norms of behaviour within the school for teachers and students.

(2) Timely detection of the forms of discrimination practiced in a particular context by either teachers or students. This is not an easy task as many forms of discrimination have become part of accepted behaviour and go unnoticed and unchallenged by the majority. Finding ways of listening to children's voices would be crucial to this exercise.

(3) Setting up a system of reporting on discriminatory practices at the school level would be a place to start. Complaint boxes that are regularly dealt with at SMC meetings is a suggested intervention.

(4) Timely redressal of instances of discrimination at the level of the school or local authority. Delays in taking action can lead to discouragement on the part of the parents and teachers.

(5) Establishing norms for classroom interactions such as seating patterns that ensure that children are not segregated on the basis of caste, community or gender.

(6) Extra-curricular activities, such as sports, music and drama with sensitivity towards participation of Dalit children, could help in breaking caste stereotype.

(7) Recognising the agency of teachers. The teachers are a key figure in the school and can help to either perpetuate or obliterate discriminatory practices. But her role in this process has been largely neglected so far.

(8) Through proper training, setting norms of teacher behaviour, strict monitoring and supervision and taking exemplary action where norms of behaviour are flouted would help enhance school inclusivity.

(9) Special effort must be made to fill the posts reserved for SC and their placement in areas with dalit concentration.

(10) Encouraging formation of and recognising, separate associations of SC teachers and expecting them to address issue relating to their service condition as well as the treatment meted out to dalit children in schools.

Q13. What are the various problems, which ST children are facing in their education?

Ans. In school as well as in higher education, those people are given special incentives who belonging to Scheduled Tribes (ST). The tribal people are spread over almost all the states barring a few states. The tribal communities are not homogeneous and are at various levels of socio-economic and educational development. Generally, a majority of the population belonging to ST community is educationally backward. Efforts are being made since independence to bring them into the mainstream of education. DPEP undertook special measures to attract students from tribal communities to enrol in nearby schools and continue until the age of school leaving stage. SSA also continued the same policy. Nevertheless, the success achieved is far from satisfactory. This issue, therefore, demands special attention.

In different parts of the country, the tribal people living have different life styles and associated problems. Generally, the problems of tribal people arise because of their isolation from the mainstream. They usually live in hilly terrains that are remote and inaccessible. Their economic status is low forcing them to send their children to work to augment family income. Tribal people use their local dialect in day to day conversations. Hence, many of the tribal students do not have adequate competence in using regional languages. Their habitation areas are not conducive to schooling. The nomadic nature of these communities forces them to move from one place to the other within the state as well as to other neighbouring states mainly in the quest of livelihood. Therefore, children, face serious problems with regard to their education, as they cannot attend a particular school throughout the year.

The problems faced by children in the tribal areas are often different from that faced by children belonging to Scheduled Castes. Hence, special interventions are needed for attracting and retaining tribal children in school. Some of the interventions, which can be considered, are:

- Textbooks in mother tongue for children at the beginning of Primary education where they do not understand regional language.
- Bridge Language Inventory for use of teachers.
- Aganwadis and Balwadis or crèches in each school in tribal areas so that the girls are not required to do baby-sitting.
- Special training for non-tribal teachers to work in tribal areas, including knowledge of tribal dialect.
- Interventions for Early Childhood Care and Education
- School/EGS like alternative facility to be set up within one kilometer of all habitations.
- Up-gradation of EGS to regular schools
- Special mainstreaming camps for out-of-school girls/ SC/ST children under the Alternative and Innovative Education component.
- Mahila Samakhya like interventions from the innovation fund.
- Provision of process-based community participation with a focus on the participation of women and SC/ST
- Provision of context specific innovative intervention for girl's education and education of SC/ST children. The innovative programmes can include: enrolment and retention drives, special camps and bridge courses, setting up special models of Alternative Schools, strengthening of madarsas and maktabs for formal education to girls, community mobilisation including setting up new working groups and working with existing working groups, monitoring attendance, remedial/coaching classes, providing a congenial learning environment inside and outside the school, etc.
- Training programme for community leaders to develop capacities for school management.
- Setting up of Block and Cluster Resource Centres for effective academic supervision.

- Free textbooks to all girls/SC/ST children up to Class-VIII.
- Mid-day-meal programme to continue as at present.
- Adequate Teaching Learning Equipment for all Primary and Upper Primary schools.
- Provision for school and teacher grants for all teachers, all children with Special needs, community-based monitoring, partnership with research and resource institutions, and periodic feedback on interventions.

Q14. Discuss the quality improvement programme for ashram schools.

Ans. In Ashram schools, a programme was under taken on the request of the Tribal Development Department of the Government of Maharashtra to improve the quality of science and mathematics education. The progamme was carried out by Homi Bhabha Centre for Science Education 1993-97 in three districts located in Shayadri ranges (western part of the state of Maharashtra). It focussed on three things: 1. Capacity building, 2. Teachers training and 3. Enhancement of child-child interaction. These things are described below:

(1) **Capacity building:** Regarding to capacity building of the school attention was given to the development of libraries and laboratories. Relevant books were made available to the library and system was set up to use them effectively. Similarly, science laboratory was strengthened with necessary equipments. In addition to develop mathematic laboratory an attempt was made.

(2) **Teacher training:** For science and mathematics teachers, six training courses were conducted over a span of three years. During these courses, the teacher were acquainted with the learning difficulties faced by the trivial students and were given guidelines on how to overcome them. For tribal children, the remedial material specially prepaid was also made available to the teachers for reference.

(3) **Enhancement of Child-child Interaction:** In the Ashram Schools, students lived together even after the class room hours. In order to make use of this time an attempt was made to enhance child-child interaction. They were suggested to undertake group activities like displaying a newspaper article on the Display Board or preparing Herbarium for the levels of nearby plant. The activities enabled them to channelise the leisure time available to them and enhanced their scholastic attainment considerably.

Q15. Discuss the educational provision of "Children with special needs".

Or

Why are children with special needs often marginalised? Mention any two reasons. [April-2016, Q.No.-29]

Ans. The objective of SSA can be achieved if the education need of every child, whatever nature he/she may be is catered. A good number of children have been found in the category of disabled with various disabilities. CWSN have often been marginalised on account of their disability, lack of awareness on the part of the parents and community about their potential. Apprehensions on the part of the teachers to teach such children also have denied them right to education. A general societal attitude of sympathy towards such children focusing more on what they cannot do rather than on what they can do has also been a barrier. Realising the importance of integrating CWSN in regular schools, SSA framework has made adequate provisions for educating CWSN.

The Sarva Siksha Abhiyan (SSA) aims to provide useful and relevant elementary education to all children including children with disabilities in the age range of 6-14 years by 2010. The person with Disability Act (1995) makes it mandatory on the part of government to provide needed educational facilities for the disabled. SSA programme lays special thrust on making education at the elementary level useful and relevant for children by improving the curricula, child centered activities and effective teaching learning strategies. It ensures that every child with special needs, irrespective of the kind, category and degree of disability, is provided education in an appropriate environment. It adopts "Zero rejection" policy so that no child is left out of the education system.

CWSN need to be facilitated to acquire certain skills that will enable them to access elementary education as envisaged in the Act. For instance, they may need mobility training, training in Braille, sign language, postural training, etc. Thus, school preparedness of children with special needs must be ensured by providing 'special training' as envisaged in the RTE Act. This training may be residential, non-residential or even home based, as per their specific requirements. The existing non-formal and alternate schooling (including home based education) options for children with disabilities can be recast as 'special training'. This means that (a) all children with special needs who are not enrolled in schools or have dropped out, will first be enrolled in a neighborhood school in an age appropriate grade, (b) they will be entitled to 'special training' through regular teachers or teachers specifically appointed for the purpose. Facilities available to CWSN in the district should be identified. Efforts to get functional and formal assessment of CWSN done should be undertaken. Special transport and other facilities required to enroll out of school CWSN in regular schools should be assessed. Data on the proportion of identified CWSN requiring aids and appliances have been provided these assistive devices through convergence with State Departments, NGOs, ADIP/ALIMCO/IEDC/other schemes, SSA funds or need to be collected other sources.

Q16. Describe the education of geographically remote children.

Ans. The Education Guarantee Scheme and Alternative and Innovative Education scheme is a part of the Sarva Shiksha Abhiyan framework.

Guidelines issued separately under the EGS & AIE shall apply. The management structure for implementation of EGS & AIE will be incorporated in the management structure of the Sarva Shiksha Abhiyan. Planning, appraisal and supervision processes will also be the same. The new scheme makes provision for diversified strategies and has flexible financial parameters. It has provided a range of options, such as EGS, Back to School Camps, Balika Shivirs, etc. The four broad focus areas are as follows:

(1) Full time community schools for small unserved habitations

(2) Mainstreaming of children through bridge courses of different duration

(3) Specific strategies for special groups like child labour, street children, adolescent girls, girls belonging to certain backward communities, children of migrating families, etc.

(4) Innovative programmes - the innovations can be in the areas of pedagogic practices, curriculum, programme management, textbooks and TLMs, etc.

All habitations not having a primary school within one kilometre and having a minimum of school age children, will be entitled to have an EGS type school. Children who have dropped out-of-school will have an opportunity to avail of bridge courses, aimed at their mainstreaming. The objective is to see the EGS and AIE as integral to the quest of UEE. For AIE and EGS, the linkages with CRC/BRC/DIET/SCERT will be required.

Among 'out of school children', there is a great heterogeneity. They could belong to remote school-less habitations, could be working children, street children, deprived children in urban slums, bonded child labourers, children of sex workers, girls belonging to the minority community, girls involved in domestic chores or sibling care, children who are engaged in cattle grazing etc. For their education, this heterogeneity demands diversified approaches and strategies.

The EGS and AIE would accord a priority to setting up of EGS centers (primary level) in unserved habitations where no school exists within a radius of 1 km and at least 15 children (and 10 in case of hilly areas) in the age group of 6-14 who are not going to schools, are available. Alternate innovative educational interventions for mainstreaming of 'out of school children' through specially designed bridge courses of different duration can be designed. Specific innovative strategies can be designed for difficult groups of children who cannot be mainstreamed, like working children, street children, adolescent girls, girls belonging to certain backward communities and children of migrant families.

Q17. Write a brief essay on urban deprived children.

Ans. As an urgent need to focus on the educational needs of deprived children in urban areas, a number of initiatives were taken to reach the urban area schools, The Municipal Corporation of larger cities were considered as "district" and Urban Slum clusters as unit of planning for purposes of preparation of Elementary Education Plans. SSA particularly emphasized on the need to work in partnership with NGOs, Municipal bodies, etc. such as the City Level Plan of Action in Calcutta (Kolkata).

It is increasingly being realised that retaining the disadvantaged children enrolled in schools is a far more challenging task than enrolling them into educational system. Around 22% children dropped out in schools is a far more challenging task than enrolling them into educational system. Around 22% children dropped out in classes I and II. Apart from adverse socio-economic conditions several factors are responsible for poor retention. The results of learning achievement surveys conducted by National Council for Education Research and Training (NCERT) and also by independent agencies highlight poor quality of learning.

A diversity of approaches is required to tackle the educational problems in urban areas. Special initiatives have to be taken for the education of deprived Urban Children, Street Children, the education of children who are rag pickers, children whose parents are engaged in professions that make children's education difficult, education of children living in urban working class slums, children who are working in industry, children working in households, children at tea shops, etc. On account of separate administrative arrangements of schools in the urban areas, there is a need to coordinate and intervene across Departments and local bodies responsible for elementary education in urban areas.

In the case of smaller towns, this calls for a provision of planning distinctively for the urban areas either as separate plans or as part of District Plans. In either case, with NGOs, municipal bodies, etc., these require partnership.

"Urban poor" refers to an important category of children which also needs special intervention and lives in urban low income areas. Urban poor children are not only economically poor, but often are deprived of family support and access to education. Children of urban poor are often excluded from education and reaching elementary education to them remains a challenge. Some of the numerous factors affecting their access to elementary education in urban areas are:

- multiplicity of administrative units,
- lack of micro level planning and coordinated implementation,
- heterogeneous community,
- ill-equipped government schools,
- disparities as reflected in the curriculum transacted in the classroom,
- poor quality of teaching,
- lack of infrastructure,
- the location and timing of the school,
- loss of earning,
- lack of authentic database on out of school children,
- severe shortage of space for opening new schools.

There are many problems related to educating the deprived urban poor children. These include lack of reliable data, inadequate schooling infrastructure, lack of incentives for deprived urban poor children to attend school, the location of schools, and so on. Although a number of NGOs have been working in the area, yet the coverage has been uneven and many have been left out. Moreover, a good proportion of these children belong to migrant families. The urban self governments have not been able to meet the challenges of reaching elementary education to this group of children. Urban poor children can be categorised in following manner:

(1) Children of migrant workers

(2) Street children

(3) Children of urban poor with disability

(4) Children in remand homes, juvenile homes, and in conflict with law

(5) Child beggars

(6) Child workers/labourers, including children working as domestic servants

(7) Children living in slums and resettlement colonies

(8) Children of sex workers

Long-term support and very individualised personal attention will be required by many of these groups. While planning for this group of children, clear focus on flexible strategies is important. Besides formal schools, SSA also provides support to out of school children in the form of Education Guarantee Scheme and other strategies under Alternative and Innovative Education programme. NGO's assistance could be effective to reach these children for government alone cannot cater to their needs. Through bridge courses, remedial courses, national open schooling programmes and back to school camps, the out of school children can also be provided education.

Q18. Write short notes on the following:

(i) Education of Working Children

Ans. The presence of child labour is one of the major concerns facing the international community. There are determined efforts to respond to the issues and at the same time arrive at progressive solutions. Child labour was utilised to varying extents through most of history, but entered public dispute with the advent of universal schooling, with changes in working conditions during the industrial revolution, and with the emergence of the concepts of workers' and children's rights.

In India, those who employ young children are punishable by law. However, the dire poverty in the house forces many children to opt for work to augment the family incomes. During school hours, these children are unable to attend regular schools as they are on work. The real solution would be see that they are taken out of work and enrolled in schools. This measure would need financial compensations for the parents which would be difficult to manage. Instead a via media can be worked out by enrolling these children in night schools.

Now-a-days, in urban areas, there are a large number of night schools. Their number in metropolitan cities is quite high and the enrolment of the students in these schools is also appreciably high. The problem with these schools is that they are forced to teach the curriculum that is meant for formal day schools. The time at the disposal of night schools teachers and students is severely limited. Moreover, these are the students who are tired of day long work. It is, therefore, necessary that a different curriculum is planned for the night school students. Since they have work experience and since they are older than formal school children they can be taught differently. Part of the education can be given through assignments that they can complete on job or during leisure time. There is no need to pressurise them to study the theoretical curriculum that the formal school students go through. Instead, the curriculum should be framed in such a way as to help them achieve life skills and to support their day to day work. Trade based training might help these student more than the formal study of facts and principles. Such a curriculum would serve the purpose of enhance their chances of higher earnings, improving their skills on job.

(ii) Education of Minority Children

Ans. The minority is constantly under the threat of assimilation. When under the compulsions of economy the family structure is loosened, the social organization faces disintegration, the handicrafts and other finer cultural traits of distinctiveness face extinction, and language remains a major identity marker if not the only one and acts as the only window to the cultural past of a people. The demand for the recognition of minority languages and their use in education, administration and mass communication draws strength from this situation.

Education is generally directed towards the needs of the students coming from homes having a majority status in the society. As a result, students belonging to minority community often feel excluded in school environment. There are following reasons for their exclusion:

(1) The preconceived notions of the students might be different from those of the majority due to difference in cultural background.

(2) Students might find the content irrelevant as they are.

(3) The language used in the textbooks and in classroom transactions could be different from the mother tongue of the students.

(4) The experiences referred to in the textbooks and in a classroom discourse might be unfamiliar to the students.

Q19. What initiatives are being taken in India to help the academic system?

Or

Write a note on 'academic support system'.

Ans. Increase in the salary, enhancement of school facilities, freedom in classroom transactions are some ways of empowerment of a practicing teacher. Some countries have set up "Teacher Support Services" to provide help to practising teachers. Teacher is expected to approach the organisation for support in his/her day to day teaching which is offered free of cost and without delay. India does not have such a support system. Nevertheless, at block and cluster levels respectively to provide support to school teachers, we have set up DIETs (District Institutes of Education and Training) and district levels and BRCs (Block Resource Centres) and CRCs (Cluster Resource Centres). At these places, practising teacher can approach resource persons and get the help that he/she needs.

Considerably, developments in technology have influenced our lives. Technology has shown us the way to increase food production, to control deadly diseases, to transport material from one place to another and to communicate with each other. School being a part of the society cannot remain aloof from the impacts of technology. The gadgets like the slide or overhead projector have entered into school system long back. In the recent years, even an LCD projector has made its headway into the school system. To deal with school subjects effectively, this projector coupled with a computer can empower teacher.

In our educational endeavour, Indian Space Research Organisation (ISRO) has come forward to help us. In October 2004, it has launched a dedicated satellite called EDUSAT. Located in the geostationary orbit this satellite is available for educational activities 24 hours a day and 365 days a year. It has brought experts and teachers close to each other. At the same time, it has brought teachers together through video conferencing to share their ideas and experiences and who work in different district or state, to get advice from those colleagues.

The world has become closer due to developments in Information Technology. It has become possible to establish fast linkages between two professionals using a world wide web. A teacher working in the remote corner of the country now has a scope to virtually interact with his/her counterparts from different parts of the world. In addition, he/she has all the information at his/her fingertips through Open Educational Resources (OER). OER suitable for students and teachers at different levels of schooling are made available free of cost. The project aims at developing suitable resources in school science and mathematics taking into accounts the needs and requirements of the system and makes it available through the MKCL website. OER material can be downloaded and used for classroom teaching without any charge. The internet facility is penetrating fast in India very fast. One can, therefore, be sure that days are not far when a typical teacher from a typical village school in India would access OER and for his/her classroom deliberations use them.

Q20. What is "inclusive education"? Define its international scenario.

Ans. Inclusive education means different and diverse students learning side by side in the same classroom. They enjoy field trips and after-school activities together. They participate in student government together. And they attend the same sports meets and plays. Inclusive education values diversity and the unique contributions each student brings to the classroom. In a truly inclusive setting, every child feels safe and has a sense of belonging. Students and their parents participate in setting learning goals and take part in decisions that affect them. And school staff have the training, support, flexibility, and resources to nurture, encourage, and respond to the needs of all students.

According to UNESCO, inclusive education is seen as "a process of addressing and responding to the diversity of needs of all learners through increasing participation in learning, cultures and communities, and reducing exclusion from education and from within education." The goal is that the whole education system will facilitate learning environments where teachers and learners embrace and welcome the challenge and benefits of diversity. Within an inclusive education approach, learning environments are fostered where individual needs are met and every student has an opportunity to succeed.

International Scenario: In recent years, the term inclusive education has gained importance. Nevertheless, in the international scenario, its origin can be traced in the history of education. Although, the inclusive education movement is now an international phenomenon, it had its origins in the relatively rich developed countries. For the disabled to the placement of such learners in regular schools these countries shifted their emphasis from special schools. This change was a part of wider movements in which disability began to be viewed no longer as a handicap that required people to be segregated from the mainstream of the society. As a result, in normal classrooms, there began the era of integration that saw the movement of inclusive education for all.

A number of international declarations are appeared with the right of child to education. The first international declaration that proclaimed this issue was Charter of the United Nations (1942). The Universal Declaration of Human Rights (1948) also reiterated the importance of right to education. Learners' right to education was enhanced further in United Nations' Declaration of Rights of child (1959). This declaration puts the responsibility of education of the child on their parents. Later, the equality of education was included in the International Covenant on Civil and Political Rights (UN, 1966). In the United Nations Convention on Rights of the Child (held in 1992) 107 countries have given formal commitment to education for all. In addition to the right of the child to education the covenant specifies that it should be on the basis of equal opportunities and directs the development of child's personality, talents, mental and physical abilities to their fullest potential. Government of India has also passed a bill for Right to Education (RTE) in the parliament, in tune with this international thinking.

Interest in the human rights of children within education policy was supported by the Salamanca Statement (UNESCO, 1994). In June 1 994, representatives of 92 governments and 25 international organisations formed the World Conference on Special Needs Education, held in Salamanca, Spain. They agreed a statement (UNESCO, 1994) on the education of all disabled children and adopted a new Framework for Action, the guiding principle of which is that ordinary schools should accommodate all children, regardless of their physical, intellectual, social, emotional, linguistic or other conditions:

"The guiding principle that informs this framework is that schools should accommodate all learners regardless of their physical, intellectual, social, emotional, linguistic or other conditions. This should include disabled and gifted learners, street and working learners, learners from remote and nomadic population, learners from linguistic, ethnic or cultural minorities and learners from other disadvantaged or marginalised areas or groups."

Q21. What are the advantages of inclusive education?

Ans. Inclusive education bears importance for developing countries more than the developed countries. These are following aspects in which practising inclusive education would prove beneficial:

The efficient use of resources: A resource intensive venture is considered as education and has to compete against other demands of the country like health care, infrastructure etc. There is therefore always a resource crunch for education in developing countries. Setting up schools for different groups of students would not be possible for these countries. Instead, for the benefit of all types of students using the limited resources would be a viable solution as it makes use of resources efficiently.

Cost effectiveness: Inclusive education is not only cost effective but also cost efficient. Inclusion promises the enhancement not only of disabled but also of non disabled learners. It thus achieves good education for all taking care of individual differences among different learners. In addition, helping to maintain harmony on different groups of the society, inclusive education acts against stratification of the society.

Decentralisation: Decentralisation is encouraged by practice of inclusive education. Decentralisation, as it is evident, allows national and local governments to reduce spending on central management, and administrative costs. At the same time, it encourages local decision making that is often close to meet the needs of the local people. It also enables local community groups to have a say in decision making. In short, it would be a consumer driven policy of education rather than a beaurocratic mode of centralised decision.

Q22. Discuss the inclusive education in respect to school and classroom.

Ans. To facilitate the development of inclusive society in which every member has an opportunity to achieve his/her potential to fullest extent is the real purpose of building an inclusive school. In order to achieve this objective, it is necessary that diversity among learner population is given due importance and provision is made to achieve everyone's rights. Access for all is the central concept in inclusive schools. It involves the psychological and physical environment of the school including curriculum transactions. All these aspects of the school should be conductive to learners with different abilities and social background. In brief, it is essential that the school should have inclusive learning environment that fosters the personal, academic and professional development of all the students.

The attitude of a teacher is the essential aspect of an inclusive classroom. A teacher who believes that the intelligence is inherited and nothing much can be done to improve it will hardly encourage the development of all the students. On the other hand, a teacher who is optimistic about the potential of individual and who maintains that the intelligence can manifest in different forms would provide an inclusive environment in the classroom to foster individual talent. Teacher must realise that diversity in learner is inevitable and everyone would have different requirements. Taking these diversities into account a teacher has to create both psychological and physical environment in the classroom. Every child has a chance to progress, in such a conducive environment.

Every year, SSA framework provides ₹1200 every disabled child. While planning for the utilisation of this money, it should be borne in mind that the amount available is not only for the use of a particular child with a special need, but also has to be utilised for planning of *Inclusive Education* activities at the school/habitat/village levels. For implementing the programme of *Inclusive Education,* the SSA State Mission Societies are allocated funds depending on the total number of disabled children identified in the district. While some disabled children may only need the help of a special education teacher, others may require simple equipment like assistive devices like hearing aid etc. However, this does not mean that this amount has to be spent annually; it can be accumulated for a year or two and utilised on a sizeable facility.

This amount could be used in other activities like assessment camps, development of training material, community awareness campaigns, 45-day Rehabilitation Council of India recognised teacher training, requesting specific services from NGOs, workshops and meetings. An attempt should be made to provide aids and appliances to identified CWSN through convergence. If this is not possible, then SSA funds could be used for this purpose. Only in exceptional circumstances, referral to residential special schools should be made. As far as possible CWSNs should be allowed stay with their family. Interventions for education of children with disabilities have to be planned by each district keeping in view available resources. In normal schools, overriding emphasis should be on inclusive education and in special schools, not isolating them.

Q23. Discuss about the protecting child rights in schools.

Ans. In March 2007, under the Commission for Protection of Child Rights Act, 2005, an Act of Parliament (Dec 2005), the National Commission for Protection of Child Rights (NCPCR) was set up. The Commission's Mandate is to ensure that all Laws, Policies, Programmes, and Administrative Mechanisms are in consonance with the Child Rights perspective as enshrined in the Constitution of India and also the UN Convention on the Rights of the Child.

According to international law, a child means every human being below the age of 18 years. This is a universally accepted definition of a child and comes from the United Nations Convention on the Rights of the Child (UNCRC), an international legal instrument accepted and ratified by most countries.India has always recognised the category of persons below the age of 18 years as distinct legal entity. That is precisely why people can vote or get a driving license or enter into legal contracts only when they attain the age of 18 years. Marriage of a girl below the age of 18 years and a boy below 21 years is restrained under the Child Marriage Restraint Act 1929. Moreover, after ratifying the UNCRC in 1992, India changed its law on juvenile justice to ensure that every person below the age of 18 years, who is in need of care and protection, is entitled to receive it from the State.

While all children need protection, because of their social, economic, or even geographical location, there are many children who are more vulnerable and need special attention than others:

- Homeless children (pavement dwellers, displaced/evicted, refugees etc.)
- Migrant children
- Street and runaway children
- Orphaned or abandoned children
- Working children
- Child beggars
- Children of prostitutes
- Trafficked children
- Children in jails/prisons
- Children affected by conflict
- Children affected by natural disasters
- Children affected by HIV/AIDS
- Children suffering from terminal diseases
- Disabled children
- Children belonging to the Scheduled Castes & Scheduled Tribes

Constitutional Guarantees that are meant specifically for children include:

- Right to free and compulsory elementary education for all children in the 6-14 year age group (Article 21 A)

- Right to be protected from any hazardous employment till the age of 14 years (Article 24)
- Right to be protected from being abused and forced by economic necessity to enter occupations unsuited to their age or strength (Article 39(e))
- Right to equal opportunities and facilities to develop in a healthy manner and in conditions of freedom and dignity and guaranteed protection of childhood and youth against exploitation and against moral and material abandonment (Article 39 (f))
- Right to early childhood care and education to all children until they complete the age of six years (Article 45)

Besides, just as any other adult male or female, children also have rights as equal citizens of India:

- Right to equality (Article 14)
- Right against discrimination (Article 15)
- Right to personal liberty and due process of law (Article 21)
- Right to being protected from being trafficked and forced into bonded labour (Article 23)
- Right of minorities for protection of their interests (Article 29)
- Right of weaker sections of the people to be protected from social injustice and all forms of exploitation (Article 46)
- Right to nutrition and standard of living and improved public health (Article 47)

Q24. What do you know about Jomtien Conference held in 1990?

Ans. The World Conference on Education for All, held from 5 to 9 March 1990 in Jomtien, Thailand, was not a single event but the start of a powerful movement. Some 1,500 participants met in Jomtien. Delegates from 155 governments, including policy-makers and specialists in education and other major sectors, together with officials and specialists representing some 20 inter governmental bodies and 150 non-governmental organisations , discussed major aspects of Education for All in 48 roundtables and a plenary commission. The Conference participants adopted the World Declaration on Education for All and a Framework for Action: Meeting Basic Learning Needs. The Declaration begins by stating that every child, youth and adult shall be able to benefit from educational opportunities designed to meet their basic learning needs. In that sense, Education for All is an expanded vision encompassing programmes, activities and services in the public and private sectors aimed at meeting the basic needs of children, youth and adults both within and outside school.

In the word conference, the participants on 'Education for All':

(1) understood that education can help ensure a safer, healthier, more prosperous and environmentally sound world.

(2) recognised that traditional knowledge and indigenous, cultural heritage have a value and validity for development.

(3) recalled that education is a fundamental right for all people of all ages, throughout our world.

(4) acknowledged that, overall the current provision of education must be made more relevant and qualitatively improved and made universally available.

(5) recognised that sound basic education is fundamental to the strengthening of higher levels of education and of scientific and technological literacy and capacity and thus to self-reliant development.

(6) knew that education was an indispensable key to, though not a sufficient condition for personal and social improvement.

Q25. Elucidate major thrusts of Jomtien Conference.

Ans. Nine articles are drafted in the conference of the World Declaration on Education according to the purpose, expanded vision, commitment and requirements for Education for All. Following are the articles related to thrusts of Jomtien conference:

Article 1: Meeting basic learning needs

(1) 'Meeting basic learning needs' stated that "every person-child, youth and adult-shall be able to benefit from educational opportunities designed to meet their basic learning needs";

(2) The satisfaction of these needs empowers individuals in any society and confers upon them a responsibility to respect and build upon their collective cultural, linguistic and spiritual heritage, to promote the education of others.

(3) Another and no less fundamental aim of educational development is the transmission and enrichment of common cultural and moral values. It is in these values that the individual and society find their identity and worth.

(4) Basic education is more than an end in itself. It is the foundation for lifelong learning and human development.

Article 2: Shaping the vision

(1) To serve the basic learning needs of all requires more than a recommitment to basic education as it now exists. What is needed is an 'expanded vision' that surpasses present resource levels, institutional structures, curricula, and conventional delivery systems while building on the best in current practices.

(2) As elaborated in Articles 3–7, the expanded vision encompasses:

Universalising access and promoting equity;

(i) Focusing on learning;

(ii) Broadening the means and scope of basic education;

(iii) Enhancing the environment for learning;

(iv) Strengthening partnerships.

(3) The realisation of an enormous potential for human progress and empowerment is contingent upon whether people can be enabled to acquire the education.

Article 3: Universalising access and promoting equity

(1) *Basic education should be provided to all children, youth and adults.* To this end, basic education services of quality should be expanded, and consistent measures must be taken to reduce disparities.

(2) For basic education to be equitable, all children, youth and adults must be given the opportunity to achieve and maintain an acceptable level of learning.

(3) The most urgent priority is to ensure access to, and improve the quality of, education for girls and women, and to remove every obstacle that hampers their active participation.

(4) An active commitment must be made to removing educational disparities. Underserved groups should not suffer any discrimination in access to learning opportunities.

(5) The learning needs of the disabled demand special attention. Steps need to be taken to provide equal access to education to every category of disabled persons as an integral part of the education system.

Article 4: Focusing on learning

Whether or not expanded educational opportunities will translate into meaningful development–for an individual or for society–depends ultimately on whether people actually learns as a result of those opportunities, i.e. whether they incorporate useful knowledge, reasoning ability, skills, and values. The focus of basic education must, therefore, be on actual learning acquisition and outcome, rather than exclusively upon enrolment, continued participation in organised programme and completion of certification requirements.

Article 5: Broadening the Means and Scope of Basic Education

The diversity, complexity, and changing nature of basic learning needs of children, youth and adults necessitates broadening and constantly redefining the scope of basic education to include the following components:

(1) Learning begins at birth.

(2) The main delivery system for the basic education of children outside the family is primary schooling.

(3) The basic learning needs of youth and adults are diverse and should be met through a variety of delivery systems.

(4) All available instruments and channels of information, communications, and social action could be used to help

convey essential knowledge and inform and educate people on social issues.

Article 6: Enhancing the environment for learning

Learning does not take place in isolation. Societies, therefore, must ensure that all learners receive the nutrition, health care, and general physical and emotional support they need in order to participate actively in and benefit from their education. Knowledge and skills that will enhance the learning environment of children should be integrated into community learning programmes for adults. The education of children and their parents or other caretakers is mutually supportive and this interaction should be used to create, for all, a learning environment of vibrancy and warmth.

Article 7: Strengthening partnership

National, regional, and local educational authorities have a unique obligation to provide basic education for all, but they cannot be expected to supply every human, financial or organizational requirement for this task. New and revitalized partnerships at all levels will be necessary: partnerships among all sub-sectors and forms of education. The recognition of the vital role of both families and teachers is particularly important. In this context, the terms and conditions of service of teachers and their status, which constitute a determining factor in the implementation of education for all, must be urgently improved in all countries

Article 8: Developing a supportive policy context

(1) In the social, cultural, and economic sectors, supportive policies are required in order to realise the full provision and utitlisation of basic education for individual and societal improvement. Suitable economic, trade, labour, employment and health policies will enhance learners' incentives and contributions to societal development.

(2) Societies should also insure a strong intellectual and scientific environment for basic education.

Article 9: Mobilising resources

(1) If the basic learning needs of all are to be met through a much broader scope of action than in the past, it will be essential to mobilise existing and new financial and human resources, public, private and voluntary.

(2) Enlarged public-sector support means drawing on the resources of all the government agencies responsible for human development.

Q26. What are the main six areas of action adopted by Jomtien Conference to meet basic needs?

Ans. To meet basic needs a framework of action was adopted in Jomtien conference these six main areas of action are stated below:

(1) Main areas of action

(i) universal access to and completion of primary education,

(ii) expansion of basic education and skill training for youth and adults,

(iii) expansion of early childhood care and development activities,

(iv) increased acquisition of knowledge, skills and values for better living by individuals and families,

(v) reduction in adult illiteracy, and

(vi) improvement in learning achievement.

(2) Five basic principles: Some basic principles for action are given in the declaration of EFA:

(i) emphasis on learning,

(ii) improvement in the learning environment,

(iii) equity: universalising access and promotion of equity,

(iv) strengthening of partnerships, and

(v) broadening of the meaning and scope of basic education.

(3) Major goals and targets: According to the action plan and basic principles to reach the goals and targets for EFA major goals and target are set.

(i) reduction in adult illiteracy rate to half its 1990 level by 2000 AD, with special emphasis on female literacy,

(ii) expansion of early childhood care and development activities, including family and community interventions, especially for the poor, disabled and the disadvantaged children,

(iii) universal access to and 80 per cent completion rate in primary education by 2000 AD, and

(iv) improvement in learning achievement such that an agreed percentage (80 per cent) of appropriate age-cohort attains or surpasses a defined level of necessary learning achievements.

(4) Impact of the Jomtien: The Jomtien conference is main contribution lies in its influence on national governments and their policies, plans and programmes. The policies and programmes of the national governments are influenced by the Jomtien conference.

(i) to give priority to EFA in their development plans

(ii) to intensify the on-going programmes of school improvement with a focus on expansion, improvement in quality, teacher training, curricular reforms, gender parity, and preferential treatment to the disadvantaged and the poor,

(iii) to broaden the scope of 'basic education' to include adult literacy, training and life skills for youth and early child care and development for pre-school age children,

(iv) to launch new projects for education development, and

(v) to formulate specific educational policies, laying a special emphasis on EFA to prepare special education plans and/or to build special components of EFA in their on-going plans.

(5) Influence on the national governments

(i) to decentralise the educational planning and management systems,

(ii) to forge partnerships between government and non-governmental organisations,

(iii) to make special efforts towards improvement in efficiency in planning and management of the education systems and

(iv) to develop mechanisms of improvement in community participation in all education activities.

(6) Initiation of special efforts

(i) to mobilise resources from the community in the form of both cash and kind, including physical and human resources for planning, management, supervision, and monitoring of schooling activities and to 'make the system work',

(ii) to enhance bilateral and regional co-operation,

(iii) to mobilise additional domestic resources by introducing tax and other fiscal reforms, and

(iv) to mobilise resources from external sources – foreign aid – from bilateral and multi-lateral sources.

Q27. Examine the impact of Jomtien Conference on E-9 countries and South Asian Regions.

Ans. Impact of Jomtien Conference on E-9 Countries

The E-9 Initiative came into being at the EFA Summit of the nine highly populated developing countries (Bangladesh, Brazil, China, Egypt, India, Indonesia, Mexico, Nigeria and Pakistan) in New Delhi, India in 1993. Representing more than half of the world's population, over two-thirds of the world's illiterate adults and over half of the world's out-of-school children, these nine countries found themselves at the time as "crucial to the achievement of the global goal of education for all' (Delhi Declaration and Framework for Action). The initiative was thus launched to enhance cooperation between and among these countries in view of strengthening their efforts "to meet the learning needs of all children, youth and adults" as agreed upon at the World Conference on Education for All (Jomtien, Thailand, 1990).

Following are the achievements in the E-9 countries as an impact of Jomtien conference:

(1) Increase in early childhood education strategies that involve parents and that support vulnerable families;

(2) Significant advance towards universal elementary education;

(3) Massive reduction in adult literacy;

(4) Improved gender equity in school access for boys and girls and for school attendance;

(5) Substantial increase in pre-school educational services;

(6) Use of distance education for the expansion of learning and for teacher training;

(7) Addressing early development of attitudes and values for co-existence and civic education;

(8) Strengthening of national database, evaluation and accreditation systems for education;

(9) Increasing public awareness for EFA through media and advocacy;

(10) Decentralisation of educational services;

(11) Expansion of partnerships with NGOs, civil society and private sector;

(12) Advance in the process of inclusion of children with special needs in mainstream schools;

(13) Development of programmes for specific target groups with appropriate inbuilt incentives; and

(14) Development of a national curriculum framework.

Impact of Jomtien Conference on South Asian Region

South Asian region means writing about one-fourth of the world's population. South Asia comprises seven contiguous countries: Bangladesh, Bhutan, India, Maldives, Nepal, Pakistan, and Sri Lanka.

Several new initiatives were made, and a wide variety of strategies, plans, programmes and projects have been prepared and executed in the countries of the South Asian region, following the Jomtien conference. Goals were reaffirmed and redefined, new goals were set, and target dates are set and reset. The progress is monitored and new interventions are designed. While many plans are prepared and quantitative target are sets.

The achievements in South Asian Regions after Jomtien are as follows:

(1) Increase in functional adult literacy

(2) Improvement in educational management information systems

(3) Increase in primary school enrolment

(4) Effective use of existing resources

(5) More partnership between the private sector and civil society

(6) Increase in the number of legislative measures, campaigns, projects and reforms in basic education

(7) Increase in functional adult literacy

(8) More innovative initiatives in basic education

(9) Higher priority given to equality

(10) Increase in national budgets for basic education

(11) Increase in 'international' assistance to basic education

Jomtien contribution has been significant in bringing all the UN agencies together to make a commitment to work for achieving EFA goals, and to support all endeavours in this regard in developing countries. Therefore, the Jomtien conference's contribution is both catalytic and direct as well.

Q28. Enumerate and explain the barriers in elementary education in developing countries.

Ans. In the whole world, about 75 million children of which more than half of them girls have no opportunity to attend primary schools. In Africa, one in three children that are enrolled in school dropout of primary education for socially disadvantaged groups. Four out of five children who do not go to school live in rural regions. Traditional role patterns inhibit enrolling girls in school in many developing countries. The stronger preference for boys in educational sector is greater in Sub-Saharan Africa, the Middle East and in South and West Asia. In addition, many children are prevented from going to school on account of crises and wars. The majority of schools have been destroyed. In many countries where civil war is raging.

In developing countries, in elementary education, the following factors have been found to be the barriers:

(1) Lack of schools and teaching staff: A comprehensive primary school network is lacking in rural regions and poor districts lack. Children in rural regions often have to walk extremely long distance to school. Many girls are not allowed to attend the schools some distance away as parents are concerned about their safety. Many schools are poorly equipped. They lack textbooks and teaching materials. For pupils, many schools have no funding for water, electricity or transport.

The working conditions of teachers are unacceptable in many developing countries many teachers have to teach two or three shifts a day in classes with very high student numbers and on poor pay. Many teachers are also poorly trained and ill-prepared in schools. Many countries in Sub-Saharan Africa also face a health problem: in some regions so many teachers have contracted AIDS those schools are forced to remain closed. Many developing countries face the problem of low-quality teaching. Teaching times and curricula are too little geared to the children's actual day-to-day reality. Life skills are not sufficiently promoted like group work, independent learning, critical thought and problem solving, the use of new technologies and the promotion.

(2) Cost of attending school: In developing countries, many people cannot afford to pay school fees or for learning materials, school uniforms and transport to school. In countries in which school fees have been abolished enrolment rates have risen markedly. Numerous families rely on the income of their children contribution. About 166 million children between the ages of 5 and 14 years have to work often up to 16 hours a day. Children have to work, i.e. one in four in Sub-Saharan Africa and one in five in Asia.

(3) Inadequate Budgets: The budgets allocated for primary education in most developing countries are too low to meet requirements to achieve the goal of universal compulsory school attendance. More money will have to be invested in the least developed countries. Bad governance, high staff turnover, inefficient use of funding, corruption and lack of management and organisational skills are other obstacles to the universal provision of education.

(4) High illiteracy rates: Some 30-50 per cent of those who leave school after four to six years of primary education are neither literate nor numerate in developing countries. Around 11 per cent of young people between the ages of 15 and 24 are classed as illiterate. In the world ninety eight percent of those who cannot read or write live in developing countries out of the total number of illiterates.

Q29. Discuss the role of international agencies in UEE.

Or

What type of the role World Bank, SIDA, DFIED are playing in UEE?

Or

Analyse the statement that the World Bank supports EFA efforts through sharing of global knowledge and good practice. [April-2016, Q.No.-30]

Ans. There are various agencies that are playing important role in UEE:

(1) UNESCO: In 1945, UNESCO was created in order to respond to the firm belief of nations, forged by two world wars in less than a generation that political and economic agreements are not enough to build a lasting peace. Peace must be established on the basis of humanity's moral and intellectual solidarity. UNESCO strives to build networks among nations that enable this kind of solidarity by mobilising for education, so that every child, boy or girl, has access to quality education as a fundamental human right and as a prerequisite for human development. Building intercultural understanding through protection of heritage and support for cultural diversity.

UNESCO helps young independent countries by providing material and human resources for educational development. It helps countries in their efforts to improve education at all level. The agency sponsors programmes to train teachers.

In the support of the 'Education For All (EFA)' movement, three UNESCO documents have been developed in support of the EFA movement:

(i) a *Plan of Action* which attempts to mobilise and rationalise action nationally, regionally and internationally;

(ii) *Guidelines for the Preparation of National Action Plans for Education for All* aiming at supporting countries in their development of national EFA plans; and

(iii) a document on *Development Partner Co-operation in the Support of Education for All: Rationale and Strategies* which forms part of the discussion in this report.

An electronic news bulletin board, set up specifically for information-sharing on EFA, provides regular updates on important events and achievements. The commitment of UNESCO to EFA is given in the following areas:

(i) to support countries in the implementation of EFA, for example in the formulation of education policies that caters to excluded groups.

(ii) to champion more efficient use of resources and increased investment in basic education.

(iii) to integrate EFA fully in all programme activities of UNESCO. This concerns education, specifically, but also inter-sectoral activities related to culture, communication and information, and the sciences.

(iv) to sustain the EFA momentum at the global level through EFA advocacy at international meetings.

(v) to develop regional mechanisms for capacity-building and exchange between countries.

(2) UNICEF: It is the leading humanitarian and development agency working globally for the rights of every child. Child rights begin with safe shelter, nutrition, protection from disaster and conflict and traverse the life cycle: pre-natal care for healthy births, clean water and sanitation, healthcare and education. UNICEF has spent over 60 years working after World War II in December, 1946 to improve the lives of children and their families. Working with and for children through adolescence and into adulthood requires a global presence whose goal is to produce results and monitor their effects. In 1953, it became a permanent part of United Nations systems. UNICEF also lobbies and partners with leaders, thinkers and policymakers to advance the access of all children to their rights–especially the most disadvantaged. UNICEF laid the foundation for growth, transformation, innovation, opportunity and equality. Whether in times of crisis or periods of peace, in cities or remote villages, it is committed to realising a fundamental, non-negotiable goal: quality education for all.

(3) World Bank: For accelerating progress toward quality, universal primary education, and other EFA goals, the World Bank supports the Education for All. In almost 90 countries worldwide the Bank supports EFA through specific operations through multidimensional efforts to:

(i) improve the dropout and retention rates of girls, as well as their learning outcomes.

(ii) protect EFA prospects in different countries.

(iii) improve primary school access and equity, as well as educational quality and learning output.

(iv) help providing education to HIV affected pupils.

(v) promote early childhood development.

On EFA goals, working with individual countries requires a mutual accountability between developing countries and donors. World Bank helps to mobilise resources needed to achieve EFA goals. The World Bank also supports EFA efforts through analytic work and the sharing of global knowledge and good practice.

(4) The Department for International Development (DFID): The Department for International Development (DFID) is a United Kingdom government department responsible for administering overseas aid. The goal of the department is "to promote sustainable development and eliminate world poverty". The main piece of legislation governing DFID's work is the International Development Act, which came into force on 17 June 2002, replacing the Overseas Development and Co-operation Act (1980). The Act makes poverty reduction the focus of DFID's work, and effectively outlaws tied aid.

Poorer states of India are supported by DFID, for example: Bihar, Madhya Pradesh, Orissa and West Bengal. DFID work with the state governments to help the poor in rural villages and urban slums earn an income and access health, education and water and sanitation services. DFID has also established Trust Funds with key multilateral partners: the World Bank, the Asian Development Bank and UNICEF. It also works with international and local NGOs and the private sector, such as the Small Industries Development Bank of India (SIDBI).

(5) Swedish International Development Cooperation Agency (SIDA): The Swedish International Development Cooperation Agency (SIDA) is a government agency working on behalf of the Swedish parliament and government, with the mission to reduce poverty in the world. Through our work and in cooperation with others, SIDA contributes to implementing Sweden's Policy for Global Development. Supporting over 2,000 projects in over 100 countries, SIDA seeks to create partnerships with companies, popular movements, organizations, universities, and government agencies for its development projects. SIDA's geographic focus is on countries in Africa, Asia, South America, and Central and Eastern Europe.

Since 1964, India has been a recipient of Swedish bilateral development assistance. The Shiksha Karmi Project (SKP) is being implemented since 1987, with assistance from the Swedish International Development Co-operation Agency (SIDA). The aim of the project is universalisation and qualitative improvement of primary education in the remote and socio-economically backward villages of Rajasthan, with primary focus on girls.

Q30. What was the world education forum, Dakar, Senegal 2000? Explain.

Or

Review the outcome of World Education Forum, Darkar, Senegal 2000.

Or

Describe in brief the issues taken up in the World Education conference at Darkar (Senegal) held in 2000.

Ans. In April 2000, more than 1,100 participants from 164 countries gathered in Dakar, Senegal, for the World Education Forum. The intention of this conference was that children, youth and adults would "benefit from educational opportunities designed to meet their basic learning needs". The World Declaration of Education for all thus defined a bold new direction in education. The decision to review progress a decade later was taken in Jomtien noted that considerable progress had been made. The report of UNESCO of the international commission on Education for the twenty First century promoted a view of education consisting four "pillars":

- learning to know
- learning to do
- learning to be
- learning to live together

Although the participants in the Forum came from diverse backgrounds, they shared a common vision. They dreamed of a world on which everyone, child and adult alike, would command the basic literacy and numeracy skills needed to function as a citizen, worker, family member and fulfilled individual in the emerging global society. The purpose of the three-day gathering was to agree on a strategy to turn this vision of 'education for all' (EFA) into a reality.

EFA Goals

(1) To expand and improve comprehensive early childhood care and education, especially for the most vulnerable and disadvantaged children;

(2) To ensure that by 2015 all children, particularly girls, children in difficult circumstances and those belonging to ethnic minorities, have access to and complete free and compulsory primary education of good quality;

(3) To ensure that the learning needs of all young people and adults are met through equitable access to appropriate learning and life skills programmes;

(4) To achieve a 50 per cent improvement in levels of adult literacy by 2015, especially for women, and equitable access to basic and continuing education for all adults;

(5) To eliminate gender disparities in primary and secondary education by 2005, and achieving gender equality in education by 2015, with a focus on ensuring girls' full and equal access to and achievement in basic education of good quality;

(6) To improve all aspects of the quality of education and ensuring excellence of all so that recognised and measurable learning outcomes are achieved by all, especially in literacy, numeracy and essential life skills.

The world education forum aims

(1) To promote EFA policies within a sustainable and well-integrated sector framework clearly linked to poverty elimination and development strategies;

(2) To implement integrated strategies for gender equality in education which recognise the need for changes in attitudes, values and practices;

(3) To mobilise strong national and international political commitment for education for all, develop national action plans and enhance significantly investment in basic education;

(4) To enhance the status, morale and professionalism of teachers;

(5) To meet the needs of education systems affected by conflict, national calamities and instability and conduct educational programmes in ways that promote mutual understanding, peace and tolerance, and help to prevent violence and conflict;

(6) To implement as a matter of urgency education programmes and actions to combat the HIV/AIDS;

(7) To systematically monitor progress towards EFA goals and strategies at the national, regional and international levels; and

(8) To harness new information and communication technologies to help achieve EFA goals.

From many countries, there is already evidence of what can be achieved through strong national strategies supported by effective development co-operation. Progress under these strategies could - and must - be accelerated through increased international support. The countries with less developed strategies must be given the support they need to achieve more rapid progress towards education for all. The participant counties will strengthen accountable international and regional mechanisms to give clear expression to these commitments and to ensure that the Dakar Framework for Action is on the agenda of every international and regional organisation, every national legislature and every local decision-making forum. The EFA 2000 Assessment highlights that the challenge of education for all is greatest in sub-Saharan Africa, in South Asia, and in the least developed countries. There will be the requirement of national, regional and international mechanisms implementation of the preceding goals and strategies to be galvanised immediately. To support the achievement of EFA, National EFA Forums will be strengthened or established. The international community will provide special technical support for those countries with significant challenges, such as complex crises or natural disasters. Read GPH books and score excellent marks.

Objective Type Questions

Q1. Identify the achievement in South-Asian Regions after Jomtien Conference:

(A) Improved gender equity in school

(B) Higher priority given to quality and innovative initiatives in basic education

(C) Massive reduction in adult illiteracy

(D) Significant advance towards universal elementary education

Ans. (B) Higher priority given to quality and innovative initiatives in basic education

Q2. ASS is a_

(A) Academic Support System

(B) Academic Success Services

(C) Advocacy Support Services

(D) Aircraft Security System

Ans. (A) Academic Support System

Q3. The idea of Four Pillars of Education was suggested by-

(A) UNICEF

(B) UNESCO

(C) NCTE

(D) UGC

Ans. (B) UNESCO

Q4. How many member states of United Nations assembled for Jomtien Conference 1990 on 'Education for All'?

(A) 145

(B) 148

(C) 150

(D) 155

Ans. (D) 155

Q5. UNESCO satellite directed television program was used first

(A) 1926

(B) 1959

(C) 1961

(D) 1965

Ans. (D) 1965

Q6. The problem of dropout in which students leave their schooling in early years can be tackled in a better way through–

(A) Reduction of the weight of curriculum

(B) Sympathy of teachers

(C) Encouragement of the students

(D) Attractive environment of the school

Ans. (C) Encouragement of the students

Q7. Which one of the following falls within an inclusive education approach?

(A) Learning environment where individual needs are met

(B) Learning environment where students rarely get opportunity to succeed

(C) Learning environment where teachers and learners maintain a distance

(D) Learning environment where indifference to challenge and benefits of diversity exist

Ans. (A) Learning environment where individual needs are met

Q8. The students belonging to the minority community often feel excluded from the school environment because

(A) they might find the content overloaded

(B) there is nothing new to learn in the school

(C) the language used in the textbooks and in classroom transactions could be different from the mother tongue

(D) they want to be a part of the mainstream

Ans. (C) the language used in the textbooks and in classroom transactions could be different from the mother tongue

Q9. Participant of Jomtien Conference reaffirmed the right of:

(A) gender Equality

(B) education for all

(C) to every citizen

(D) education HIV/AIDS affected child

Ans. (B) education for all

Q10. E-9 countries means-

(A) Electronic countries

(B) Economical advance countries

(C) High population countries

(D) Economical backward countries

Ans. (C) High population countries

Q11. The objective of Inclusive Education is

(A) to uncover and minimise barriers to learning

(B) to change attitudes, behaviours, teaching methods, curricular and environments to meet the needs of all children

(C) to promote constantly the local cultures and contents of various communities of the society

(D) All the above

Ans. (D) All the above

Q12. Special education is related to

(A) Educational for talented students

(B) Educational programmes for disabled students

(C) Training programmes for Teachers

(D) Training programmes for retarded

Ans. (B) Educational programmes for disabled students

Q13. Inclusive education refers to a school education system that

(A) emphasised the need to promote the education of the girl child only

(B) includes children with disability

(C) includes children regardless of physical, intellectual, social, linguistic or other differently able conditions

(D) encourages education of children with special needs through exclusive schools

Ans. (C) includes children regardless of physical, intellectual, social, linguistic or other differently able conditions

Q14. Special needs education is the type of education:

(A) given to very special students

(B) given to students with disabilities

(C) provided to intelligent students

(D) established by colonial masters

Ans. (B) given to students with disabilities

Q15. Students of disadvantaged groups should be taught along with the normal students. It implies

(A) Inclusive Education

(B) Special Education

(C) Integrated Education

(D) Exclusive Education

Ans. (A) Inclusive Education

Q16. Article 45 under the Indian Constitution, provides for

(A) Rights of minorities to establish educational institutions

(B) Right to early childhood care and education to all children

(C) Education for weaker sections of the country

(D) Giving financial assistance to less advanced states

Ans. (B) Right to early childhood care and education to all children

Q17. What is the biggest advantage of interaction between the teacher and the students?

(A) It encourages the students to ask questions

(B) It facilitates effective learning

(C) It results in better group relations

(D) It satisfies the teacher

Ans. (B) It facilitates effective learning

Q18. Reflective Practice refers to-

(A) taking action to improve on what one has learned

(B) teacher's ability to look at every aspect of her/his teaching critically

(C) recalling or detailing salient events

(D) helpful feelings and removing or containing obstructive ones

Ans. (A) taking action to improve on what one has learned

Q19. Among the scheduled castes of India, which is the main cause of social mobility?

(A) Migration

(B) Education

(C) Political awakening

(D) Television

Ans. (B) Education

Q20. Today, the majority of students with disabilities are:

(A) educated in general education classrooms for at least a portion of the school day.

(B) fully integrated into general education classrooms for the entire school day.

(C) taught in self-contained classrooms

(D) taught in separate schools

Ans. (A) educated in general education classrooms for at least a portion of the school day.

Q21. Five major programs through which UNESCO pursues its objectives includes

(A) education and culture

(B) natural sciences

(C) social sciences

(D) all of above

Ans. (A) education and culture

Q22. The inclusions of SC children in school are:

(A) Textbooks in mother tongue for children at the beginning of primary education where they do not understand regional language

(B) Special mainstreaming camps for out-of-school children under the Alternative and Innovative Education component

(C) Establishing norms of behaviour within the school for teachers, school staff and students

(D) Bridge Language Inventory for use of teachers

Ans. (C) Establishing norms of behaviour within the school for teachers, school staff and students

Q23. What is/are the special problem(s) of the deprived children of urban areas in the field of education?

(A) The education of street children

(B) The education of children who are rag pickers

(C) Children whose parents are engaged in professions that make children's education difficult

(D) All of the above

Ans. (D) All of the above

Q24. The National Commission for Protection of Child Rights (NCPCR) was set up in-

(A) March 2006

(B) March 2007

(C) March 2008

(D) March 2009

Ans. (B) March 2007

☺☺☺

Question Papers

DIPLOMA IN ELEMENTARY EDUCATION (D.EL.ED.)
Elementary Education in India: A Socio-Cultural Perspective (501)
April, 2016

General Instructions:

(a) All question are compulsory.

(b) There are total 42 questions in this paper.

(c) (i) Question Nos. 1 to 15 are multiple choice-type questions having 1 mark each.

(ii) Question Nos. 16 to 30 are very short answer-type questions having 1 mark each.

(iii) Question Nos. 31 to 40 are short answer-type questions having 2 marks each.

(iv) Questions Nos. 41 and 42 are long answer-type questions having 10 marks each.

Q1. Which one of the following is not a salient feature of the National Policy on Education, 1986?

(A) Military training for national defence

(B) Promotion of adult education

(C) Equal educational opportunities for all

(D) Accountability to education

निम्नलिखित में से कौन-सा, राष्ट्रीय शिक्षा नीति, 1986 का एक प्रमुख लक्षण नहीं है?

(A) राष्ट्रीय सुरक्षा के लिए सैनिक प्रशिक्षण

(B) प्रौढ़ शिक्षा को प्रोत्साहन

(C) सभी को शिक्षा के समान अवसर

(D) शिक्षा में उत्तरदायित्व

Ans. (A) Military training for national defence

Q2. Education can accelerate the process of modernisation by

(A) raising the salaries of teachers

(B) emphasising teaching of vocational subjects and science

(C) introducing common school system of public education

(D) presenting before students high ideas of social justice

शिक्षा किस प्रकार आधुनिकीकरण की प्रक्रिया को त्वरित कर सकती है?

(A) अध्यापकों का वेतन बढ़ाकर

(B) व्यावसायिक विषयों एवं विज्ञान के शिक्षण पर बल देकर

(C) सार्वजनिक शिक्षा की सामूहिक विद्यालय प्रणाली को लागू करके

(D) विद्यार्थियों के समक्ष सामाजिक न्याय के उच्च आदर्श प्रस्तुत करके

Ans. (B) emphasising teaching of vocational subjects and science

Q3. Which one of the following rights is an obstacle in the healthy and free growth of the children?

(A) Freedom of thought

(B) Freedom of choice

(C) Freedom of spending

(D) Freedom of speech

बच्चों के स्वस्थ एवं स्वतंत्र विकास में निम्नलिखित में से कौन-सा अधिकार बाधक है?

(A) विचार की स्वतंत्रता

(B) चयन की स्वतंत्रता

(C) व्यय की स्वतंत्रता

(D) भाषण/बोलने की स्वतंत्रता

Ans. (C) Freedom of spending

Q4. Which one of the following is a function of DIET?

(A) To carry out current repairs of school buildings

(B) Training and orientation of instructors and supervisors of non-formal education

(C) To arrange mid-day meal wherever possible

(D) To manage and distribute school's finances

निम्नलिखित में से कौन-सा, **DIET** का प्रकार्य है?

(A) विद्यालय भवनों की वर्तमान कालीन मरम्मत कराते रहना

(B) गैर-औपचारिक शिक्षा के इंस्ट्रक्टरों तथा पर्यवेक्षकों का प्रशिक्षण तथा अभिमुखीकरण

(C) जहाँ भी संभव हो, मध्याह्न भोजन की व्यवस्था करना

(D) विद्यालयों में वित्त प्रबंधन तथा वितरण

Ans. (B) Training and orientation of instructors and supervisors of non-formal education

Q5. SIEMAT performs the function of dissemination of knowledge through

(A) compilation of case studies

(B) institutional planning

(C) seminars and discussions

(D) technical support

एस.आई.ई.एम.ए.टी. (SIEMAT) ज्ञान का प्रचार (विस्तार) करने का कार्य करता है–

(A) केस अध्ययनों के संकलन द्वारा

(B) संस्थागत नियोजन द्वारा

(C) सेमीनारों तथा चर्चाओं द्वारा

(D) तकनीकी सहायता द्वारा

Ans. (C) seminars and discussions

Q6. Which one of the following is a non-formal education programme to cater to the needs of working children?

(A) Madrassa

(B) Balak and Balika Shikshan Shivir

(C) Muktangan

(D) Sahaj Shiksha Kendra

निम्नलिखित में से कौन-सा कार्यक्रम कार्यरत बच्चों की आवश्यकताओं की पूर्ति के लिए एक गैर-औपचारिक शिक्षा कार्यक्रम है?

(A) मदरसा

(B) बालक तथा बालिका शिक्षण शिविर

(C) मुक्तांगन

(D) सहज शिक्षा केंद्र

Ans. (D) Sahaj Shiksha Kendra

Q7. The combination of primary and upper primary schooling is termed as

(A) elementary education

(B) universalisation of education

(C) secondary education

(D) pre-basic education

प्राथमिक तथा उच्च प्राथमिक शिक्षा को सामूहिक रूप से क्या कहा जाता है?

(A) प्रारंभिक शिक्षा

(B) शिक्षा का सार्विकीकरण

(C) माध्यमिक शिक्षा

(D) प्री-बेसिक शिक्षा

Ans. (A) elementary education

Q8. The funds provided under 'Research and Evaluation' in SSA can be utilised for

(A) government schools only
(B) aided schools only
(C) both government and aided schools
(D) un-aided schools only

सर्व शिक्षा अभियान में 'अनुसंधान व मूल्यांकन' के अंतर्गत प्रावधानित निधियों को इस्तेमाल किया जा सकता है–

(A) केवल सरकारी स्कूलों के लिए
(B) केवल सहायता-प्राप्त स्कूलों के लिए
(C) सरकारी एवं सहायता-प्राप्त स्कूलों के लिए
(D) केवल सहायता रहित स्कूलों के लिए

Ans. (C) both government and aided schools

Q9. Under SSA, funds will be transferred to VECs/SMCs/ Gram Panchayats for

(A) maintenance and repair of schools
(B) upgradation of schools
(C) salary of teachers
(D) Both (A) and (B)

सर्व शिक्षा अभियान के अंतर्गत, निधियों को VECs/SMCs/ग्राम पंचायतों के पास हस्तांतरित किया जाएगा–

(A) स्कूलों के रखरखाव व मरम्मत के लिए
(B) स्कूलों में सुधार के लिए
(C) अध्यापकों के वेतन के लिए
(D) (A) तथा (B) दोनों

Ans. (D) Both (A) and (B)

Q10. Which one of the following is considered outside the category of basic amenities?

(A) Housing
(B) Education
(C) Television
(D) Electricity

निम्नलिखित में से किसको आधारभूत सुविधाओं की श्रेणी से बाहर गिना जाता है?

(A) आवास
(B) शिक्षा
(C) टेलीविजन
(D) बिजली

Ans. (C) Television

Q11. RTE conceives a vibrant partnership with NGOs in the area of

(A) developing traditional pedagogy

(B) expressing moral concerns

(C) inculcating scientific attitude

(D) capacity building

शिक्षा के अधिकार की अवधारणा के अनुसार गैर-सरकारी संस्थाओं के साथ सक्रिय साझेदारी का क्षेत्र कौन-सा है?

(A) पारंपरिक शिक्षा प्रणाली का विकास

(B) नैतिक सरोकारों की अभिव्यक्ति

(C) वैज्ञानिक दृष्टिकोण पैदा करना

(D) क्षमता निर्माण

Ans. (D) capacity building

Q12. Which one of the following statements about core planning team is false?

(A) Involving a core planning team gives legitimacy to the plan

(B) Teachers can also collect all the required information for planning

(C) The community will feel a sense of ownership by forming such a team

(D) The representatives of the community contribute positively while taking decisions about priorities

आभ्यंतर (कोर) आयोजन दल से संबंधित कौन-सा कथन असत्य है?

(A) आभ्यंतर योजना दल को सम्मिलित करना योजना को वैधता प्रदान करता है

(B) योजना के लिए आवश्यक सभी सूचनाओं को अध्यापक भी एकत्र कर सकते हैं

(C) ऐसे दल के निर्माण से समुदाय में स्वामित्व की भावना जागृत होती है

(D) समुदाय के प्रतिनिधि प्राथमिकताओं पर निर्णय लेने में सकारात्मक योगदान देते हैं

Ans. (B) Teachers can also collect all the required information for planning

Q13. Quality of education is primarily concerned with

(A) quality of life in all its dimensions

(B) marks gained in examinations

(C) memorisation

(D) learning of English

शिक्षा की गुणवत्ता मूलतः संबद्ध है–

(A) अपने सभी आयामों में, जीवन की गुणवत्ता से

(B) परीक्षाओं में मिले प्राप्तांकों से

(C) कंठस्थ करने से

(D) अंग्रेजी सीखने से

Ans. (A) quality of life in all its dimensions

Q14. The students belonging to the minority community often feel excluded from the school environment because

(A) they might find the content overloaded

(B) there is nothing new to learn in the school

(C) the language used in the textbook and in classroom transactions could be different from their mother tongue

(D) they want to be a part of the mainstream

अल्पसंख्यक वर्ग के विद्यार्थी प्रायः अपने आपको विद्यालयी पर्यावरण से बाहर अनुभव करते हैं क्योंकि–

(A) शायद उन्हें विषयवस्तु बहुत बोझिल लगती है

(B) स्कूल में सीखने योग्य कुछ नया ही नहीं होता है

(C) पुस्तक की भाषा तथा कक्षा में प्रयोग की जाने वाली भाषा, उनकी मातृभाषा से भिन्न होती है

(D) वे मुख्य धारा का एक हिस्सा बनना चाहते हैं

Ans. (C) the language used in the textbook and in classroom transactions could be different from their mother tongue

Q15. How many member states of United Nations assembled for Jomtien Conference 1990 on 'Education for All'?

(A) 145

(B) 148

(C) 150

(D) 155

'सभी के लिए शिक्षा' पर हुए जॉमेतियन सम्मेलन, 1990 के लिए संयुक्त राष्ट्र के कितने सदस्य देशों ने मिलकर सभा की?

(A) 145

(B) 148

(C) 150

(D) 155

Ans. (D) 155

Q16. Who proposed national framework for curriculum and for what purpose?

राष्ट्रीय पाठ्यचर्या रूपरेखा की कल्पना किसने की थी और किस उद्देश्य से?

Ans. Refer to Chapter-1, Q.No.-18

Q17. Mention any one advantage of free and compulsory education.

निःशुल्क तथा अनिवार्य शिक्षा के किसी एक लाभ का उल्लेख कीजिए।

Ans. Advantage of free and compulsory education is providing education to all children of 6 to 14 years.

Q18. What is the duty of a headmaster from whose school a child is required to move to another school?

उस मुख्य अध्यापक का क्या कर्त्तव्य बनता है जिसके विद्यालय का एक विद्यार्थी उस विद्यालय को छोड़कर किसी अन्य विद्यालय में जाना चाहता है?

Ans. The headmaster should extend every help to the child who needs to get transferred. S/he is expected to issue the transfer certificate to the child. Delay in issuance of transfer certificate shall be liable for disciplinary action under the service rules applicable to himher.

Q19. Mention any one role of the teacher under RTE Act.

शिक्षा का अधिकार अधिनियम के अंतर्गत अध्यापक की किसी एक भूमिका का उल्लेख कीजिए।

Ans. Refer to Chapter-1, Q.No.-26

Q20. Justify organising orientation programmes by SCERT.

एस.सी.ई.आर.टी. **(SCERT)** द्वारा आयोजित किए जाने वाले अभिमुखीकरण कार्यक्रमों का औचित्य स्थापित कीजिए।

Ans. Refer to Chapter-1, Q.No.-34

Q21. Write the main objective of the Matriprabodhan Project.

मातृ-प्रबोधन परियोजना का मुख्य उद्देश्य लिखिए।

Ans. Refer to Chapter-2, Q.No.-7

Q22. Calculate the gross enrollment ratio (GER) in percent if the number of children enrolled in a primary school is 75 and the number of children of primary school age is 50.

सकल पंजीयन अनुपात **(GER)** का प्रतिशत में परिकलन कीजिए यदि किसी प्राथमिक विद्यालय में पंजीकृत बच्चों की संख्या 75 हो तथा प्राथमिक विद्यालय आयु

वर्ग के कुल बच्चों की संख्या 50 हो।

Ans. The number of children enrolled in a primary school = 75

The number of children of primary school age = 50

Gross Enrollment Ration (GER) =

$$\text{Primary GER} = \frac{\text{Number of children eurolled in primary school}}{\text{Number of children of primary school age}}$$

$$= \frac{75}{50} = 1.5$$

Hence, percentage of GER = GER×100
= 1.5×100
=150 percent (approx)

Q23. Who launched the Sarva Shiksha Abhiyan and when?

सर्व शिक्षा अभियान किसने प्रारंभ किया और कब?

Ans. Refer to Chapter-2, Q.No.-11

Q24. Who supports the salary of teachers appointed under the SSA programme?

सर्व शिक्षा अभियान कार्यक्रम के अंतर्गत नियुक्त किए अध्यापकों को वेतन कौन देता है?

Ans. Refer to Chapter-2, Q.No.-15

Q25. How does SSA make education at the elementary level useful and relevant to the children?

सर्व शिक्षा अभियान किस प्रकार प्राथमिक स्तर की शिक्षा को बच्चों के लिए उपयोगी तथा प्रासंगिक बना देता है?

Ans. Refer to Chapter-2, Q.No.-13

Q26. What is meant by micro-planning?

सूक्ष्म-आयोजन से क्या अभिप्राय है?

Ans. Refer to Chapter-2, Q.No.-21

Q27. How can we achieve the goal of decentralised elementary education?

विकेंद्रित प्रारंभिक शिक्षा का लक्ष्य कैसे प्राप्त किया जा सकता है?

Ans. Refer to Chapter-2, Q.No.-19

Q28. Mention any two core components of quality in education.

शिक्षा में गुणवत्ता के किन्हीं दो आभ्यंतर (अनिवार्य) घटकों का उल्लेख कीजिए।

Ans. Refer to Chapter-3, Q.No.-1

Q29. Why are children with special needs often marginalised? Mention any two reasons.

विशेष आवश्यकता वाले बच्चों को प्राय: हाशिए पर क्यों रखा जाता है? किन्हीं दो कारणों का उल्लेख कीजिए।

Ans. Refer to Chapter-3, Q.No.-15

Q30. Analyse the statement that the World Bank supports EFA efforts through sharing of global knowledge and good practice.

इस कथन का विश्लेषण कीजिए कि विश्व बैंक वैश्विक ज्ञान तथा अच्छी पद्धतियों में सम्मिलित होने का अवसर प्रदान करके EFA (सभी को शिक्षा) के प्रयासों में सहायता करता है।

Ans. Refer to Chapter-3, Q.No.-29

Q31. Mention any two recommendations of the National Committee on Women Education, 1958.

महिला शिक्षा पर राष्ट्रीय समिति, 1958 की किन्हीं दो सिफारिशों का उल्लेख कीजिए।

Ans. Refer to Chapter-1, Q.No.-11

Q32. The NCF, 2005 is based on which of our guiding principles?

राष्ट्रीय पाठ्यचर्या रूपरेखा (NCF), 2005 हमारे किन निर्देशक सिद्धांतों पर आधारित है?

Ans. Refer to Chapter-1, Q.No.-19

Q33. Examine the scope of participation by the children under their right to participate.

भागीदारी के अधिकार के अंतर्गत, बच्चों द्वारा भागीदारी की संभावनाओं का परीक्षण कीजिए।

Ans. The physical, mental, social and emotional needs of the young child can be met through Right to Participation. Every child's Participation is unique. Children's participation is children's empowerment. Hence,

Participation in Early Childhood Care and Development plays a crucial role and it has to be ensured and strengthened.

Q34. Highlight the levels and areas of teacher training being organised by NCERT.

एन.सी.ई.आर.टी. (NCERT) द्वारा आयोजित किए जा रहे शिक्षक प्रशिक्षण के स्तरों तथा क्षेत्रों को उजागर कीजिए।

Ans. Refer to Chapter-1, Q.No.-32

Q35. Mention the four major aims of NCERT.

एन.सी.ई.आर.टी. (NCERT) के चार मुख्य उद्देश्यों का उल्लेख कीजिए।

Ans. Refer to Chapter-1, Q.No.-31

Q36. Describe any two strategies adopted in Uttar Pradesh Basic Education Project.

उत्तर प्रदेश की बेसिक शिक्षा परियोजना द्वारा अपनाई गई किन्हीं दो कार्यनीतियों का वर्णन कीजिए।

Ans. Refer to Chapter-2, Q.No.-2

Q37. Explain any two main aims of education.

शिक्षा के किन्हीं दो मुख्य उद्देश्यों की व्याख्या कीजिए।

Ans. Two aims of education are as follows:

(i) To provide men and women with minimum of the skill necessary for them to take their place in the society; and

(ii) To seek further knowledge, i.e. it enables us to develop critical outlook.

Q38. Give any two examples of the lessons/topics which can be taught more effectively if children are taken outside the class.

ऐसे किन्हीं दो पाठों अथवा विषयों के उदाहरण दीजिए जिन्हें अधिक प्रभावी तरीके से पढ़ाया जा सकता है यदि बच्चों को कक्षा से बाहर ले जाया जाए।

Ans. Refer to Chapter-1, Q.No.-19

Q39. How far is it justified to say that 'open-mindedness' is a key component of the reflective practice advocated by John Dewey?

यह कहना कहाँ तक उचित है कि 'खुली मानसिकता' जॉन ड्यूवी द्वारा प्रतिपादित विमर्शी प्रक्रिया का एक महत्त्वपूर्ण घटक है?

Ans. Refer to Chapter-3, Q.No.-8

Q40. Describe any two factors which act as barriers in elementary education in developing countries.

विकासशील देशों में प्राथमिक शिक्षा के मार्ग में बाधक बनने वाले किन्हीं दो कारकों का वर्णन कीजिए।

Ans. Refer to Chapter-3, Q.No.-28

Q41. Describe the role and responsibilities of Guru under the Gurukul system.

गुरुकुल प्रणाली के अंतर्गत गुरु की भूमिका तथा उत्तरदायित्वों का वर्णन कीजिए।

Ans. Refer to Chapter-1, Q.No.-2

Q42. What is your opinion about employing young children? Why are they unable to attend regular schools? What type of curriculum should be framed to educate such children?

छोटे बच्चों को काम पर भेजने के बारे में आपकी क्या राय है? वे नियमित विद्यालयों में भर्ती क्यों नहीं हो सकते? ऐसे बच्चों को शिक्षित करने के लिए किस प्रकार की पाठ्यचर्या बनाई जानी चाहिए?

Ans. Refer to Chapter-3, Q.No.-18 (i)

☺☺☺

"A Man without Education is like a Building without Foundation"

DIPLOMA IN ELEMENTARY EDUCATION (D.EL.ED.)

Elementary Education in India: A Socio-Cultural Perspective (501)

October, 2016

General Instructions:

(a) All question are compulsory.

(b) There are total 42 questions in this paper.

(c) (i) Question Nos. 1 to 15 are multiple choice-type questions having 1 mark each.

(ii) Question Nos. 16 to 30 are very short answer-type questions having 1 mark each.

(iii) Question Nos. 31 to 40 are short answer-type questions having 2 marks each.

(iv) Questions Nos. 41 and 42 are long answer-type questions having 10 marks each.

Q1. Which one of the following statements is true with respect to total homework time prescribed by NCF, 2005?

(A) Two hours a day up to Class VIII

(B) No homework up to Class II

(C) Three hours a day in secondary classes

(D) Four hours a day in classes higher than secondary

राष्ट्रीय पाठ्यचर्या की रूपरेखा, 2005 के आधार पर गृह-कार्य के लिए निर्धारित समय हेतु निम्न में से कौन-सा वाक्य सही है?

(A) कक्षा आठ तक 2 घंटा प्रतिदिन

(B) कक्षा दो तक कोई गृह-कार्य नहीं

(C) माध्यमिक कक्षाओं में 3 घंटा प्रतिदिन

(D) उच्चतर-माध्यमिक कक्षाओं में 4 घंटा प्रतिदिन

Ans. (B) No homework up to Class II

Q2. For achieving the goal of education for increasing productivity, Kothari Commission had suggested

(A) introducing SUPW as an integral part of general education

(B) adopting new methods of teaching

(C) developing all modern Indian languages

(D) introducing moral, social and spiritual values

कोठारी आयोग ने शिक्षा की उत्पादकता वृद्धि के मुख्य लक्ष्य को साकार करने हेतु क्या सुझाव दिया था?

(A) सामाजिक रूप से उपयोगी उत्पादक कार्य (एस.यू.पी.डब्ल्यू.) को सामान्य शिक्षा के एक अभिन्न भाग के रूप में रखना

(B) शिक्षण की नई विधियों को अपनाना

(C) सभी आधुनिक भाषाओं को विकसित करना

(D) नैतिक, सामाजिक तथा आध्यात्मिक मूल्यों को सन्निविष्ट करना

Ans. (A) introducing SUPW as an integral part of general education

Q3. Which one of the following statements best describes the duties of a teacher?

(A) Maintain regularity and punctuality

(B) Motivate the parents for enrollment of children

(C) Complete the curriculum within specific time

(D) All of the above

निम्नलिखित में से कौन-सा वाक्य अध्यापक के कर्त्तव्यों को सर्वोत्तम दर्शाता है?

(A) नियमितता और समयबद्धता

(B) अभिभावकों को अभिप्रेरित करना ताकि वे बच्चों का पंजीयन कराएँ

(C) निर्धारित समय में पाठ्यचर्या को पूरा करना

(D) उपरोक्त सभी

Ans. (D) All of the above

Q4. Which one of the following is an overarching function of DIETS?

(A) Training and orientation of various target groups

(B) Academic resource support to elementary education system

(C) Action research and experimentation

(D) All of the above

निम्नलिखित में से कौन-सा डाइट्स के कार्यों को सर्वोत्तम प्रदर्शित करता है?

(A) विभिन्न लक्ष्य-समूहों का प्रशिक्षण तथा अभिमुखीकरण

(B) प्रारंभिक शिक्षा प्रणाली को शैक्षिक समर्थन

(C) क्रियात्मक शोध तथा प्रयोगीकरण

(D) उपरोक्त सभी

Ans. (D) All of the above

Q5. SIEMAT is directly concerned with

(A) teachers

(B) educational planners and administrators

(C) parents

(D) children

निम्नलिखित में से किसके लिए एस.आई.ई.एम.ए.टी. की प्रत्यक्ष भूमिका है?

(A) अध्यापक

(B) शैक्षिक नियोजक एवं प्रशासक

(C) अभिभावक

(D) शिक्षार्थी/स्कूली छात्र-छात्राएँ

Ans. (B) educational planners and administrators

Q6. The objective of the Lok Jumbish Project was to achieve education for all by the year

(A) 1995

(B) 2000

(C) 2010

(D) 2015

लोक जुम्बिश प्रोजेक्ट का उद्देश्य सबके लिए शिक्षा को प्राप्त करना था–

(A) वर्ष 1995 तक

(B) वर्ष 2000 तक

(C) वर्ष 2010 तक

(D) वर्ष 2015 तक

Ans. (B) 2000

Q7. Bihar Education Project (BEP) was initiated in 1991-92 in

(A) 3 districts

(B) 4 districts

(C) 5 districts

(D) 6 districts

बिहार शिक्षा परियोजना (BEP) 1991-92 में शुरू की गई–

(A) 3 जिलों में

(B) 4 जिलों में

(C) 5 जिलों में

(D) 6 जिलों में

Ans. (A) 3 districts

Q8. Which one of the following is proposed as an activity under the intervention 'Research and Evaluation' under SSA?

(A) Training of teachers

(B) Planning and implementation

(C) Providing regular generation of community-based data

(D) Strengthening of resource groups

सर्व शिक्षा अभियान के अंतर्गत 'शोध तथा मूल्यांकन' संबंधी घटक में निम्नलिखित में से किस गतिविधि को सम्मिलित किया गया है?

(A) अध्यापकों का प्रशिक्षण

(B) योजना बनाना तथा उसे कार्यान्वित करना

(C) नियमित रूप से समुदाय-आधारित आँकड़े एकत्रित करना

(D) संसाधन समूहों का सुदृढ़ीकरण

Ans. (C) Providing regular generation of community-based data

Q9. Identify the objective of harmonisation of the RTE Act, 2009 and SSA:

(A) To assess the attitude of children with special needs towards special teachers

(B) To assess the attitude of normal students towards inclusion of children with special needs

(C) To analyse the relationship between the teachers and the students

(D) To certify the nature of disability of the children with special needs

शिक्षा का अधिकार अधिनियम, 2009 तथा सर्व शिक्षा अभियान के सुमेलीकरण के उद्देश्य की पहचान कीजिए–

(A) विशेष आवश्यकता वाले बच्चों के अपने विशिष्ट अध्यापकों के प्रति दृष्टिकोण का आकलन करना

(B) विशेष आवश्यकता वाले बच्चों को सामान्य बच्चों के साथ मिलाए जाने पर सामान्य बच्चों के दृष्टिकोण का आकलन करना

(C) अध्यापकों तथा विद्यार्थियों के बीच संबंधों का विश्लेषण करना

(D) विशेष आवश्यकता वाले बच्चों की अक्षमता की प्रकृति को प्रमाणित करना

Ans. (B) To assess the attitude of normal students towards inclusion of children with special needs

Q10. Which vital aspect of teaching-learning process takes place outside the class?

(A) Display of materials and usability

(B) Seating arrangement

(C) Using electronic media

(D) Familiarisation of bio-diversity

अध्यापन-अधिगम प्रक्रिया का कौन-सा महत्त्वपूर्ण पक्ष कक्षा के बाहर संचालित होता है?

(A) पाठ्य सामग्री का प्रदर्शन तथा इनकी प्रयोज्यता

(B) बैठने की व्यवस्था

(C) इलेक्ट्रॉनिक मीडिया का प्रयोग

(D) जैविक विविधता से परिचय कराना

Ans. (D) Familiarisation of bio-diversity

Q11. RTE conceives a vibrant partnership with NGOs in the area of

(A) assessing the functioning of RTE

(B) conducting the programmes to improve discipline

(C) promoting the teachers

(D) expressing gender concerns

शिक्षा का अधिकार अवधारणा में एन.जी.ओ. के साथ सक्रिय सहभागिता का क्षेत्र कौन-सा है?

(A) 'शिक्षा के अधिकार' कार्यान्वयन का आकलन करना

(B) अनुशासनात्मक सुधार संबंधी प्रोग्रामों को चलाना

(C) अध्यापकों को प्रोन्नत करना

(D) जेंडर (लिंग) संबंधी सरोकारों को उजागर करना

Ans. (D) expressing gender concerns

Q12. Appraisal of the district plan before it is finalised involves

(A) evidence based on real situation

(B) convincing justification of needs

(C) financial-technical feasibility of plan

(D) All of the above

अंतिम रूप दिए जाने से पूर्व जिला योजनाओं के मूल्यनिर्धारण के लिए जानना आवश्यक है–

(A) साक्ष्य के रूप में दिए जाने वाले आँकड़े वास्तविक स्थिति पर आधारित हैं

(B) आवश्यकताओं का औचित्य युक्तियुक्त है

(C) प्रस्तावित योजना वित्तीय तथा तकनीकी रूप से व्यवहार्य है

(D) उपरोक्त सभी

Ans. (D) All of the above

Q13. The education system in India does not encourage

(A) memorisation of textbooks

(B) those who score the most

(C) values, principles and life skills

(D) answering according to the prescribed textbook

भारतीय शिक्षा प्रणाली निम्नलिखित में से किसको प्रोत्साहन नहीं देती?

(A) पाठ्य-पुस्तकों को रटने को

(B) अधिक अंक प्राप्त करने वालों को

(C) मूल्यों, सिद्धांतों तथा जीवन कौशलों को

(D) पाठ्य-पुस्तकों की विषय-वस्तु के अनुसार ही उत्तर देने को

Ans. (A) memorisation of textbooks

Q14. Which one of the following falls within an inclusive education approach?

(A) Learning environment where individual needs are met

(B) Learning environment where students rarely get opportunity to succeed

(C) Learning environment where teachers and learners maintain a distance

(D) Learning environment where indifference to challenge and benefits of diversity exist

निम्नलिखित में से कौन-सा उपागम, समावेशी शिक्षा के अंतर्गत आता है?

(A) सीखने के लिए ऐसा वातावरण जहाँ विद्यार्थियों की व्यक्तिगत आवश्यकताएँ पूरी होती हैं

(B) सीखने के लिए ऐसा वातावरण जहाँ शायद ही कभी विद्यार्थियों को सफल होने का अवसर प्राप्त होता है

(C) सीखने के लिए ऐसा वातावरण जहाँ शिक्षक तथा शिक्षार्थी एक-दूसरे से अंतर बनाए रखते हों

(D) सीखने के लिए ऐसा वातावरण जहाँ चुनौतियों तथा विभिन्नता के लाभों के प्रति उदासीनता हो

Ans. (A) Learning environment where individual needs are met

Q15. Identify the achievement in South-Asian Regions after Jomtien Conference:

(A) Improved gender equity in school

(B) Higher priority given to quality and innovative initiatives in basic education

(C) Massive reduction in adult illiteracy

(D) Significant advance towards universal elementary education

जॉमेतियन सम्मेलन के पश्चात् दक्षिण एशिया क्षेत्र की उपलब्धि को पहचानिए–

(A) विद्यालयों में लैंगिक समानता में सुधार

(B) बेसिक शिक्षा में गुणवत्ता तथा नवाचारी पहलों को प्राथमिकता

(C) प्रौढ़ निरक्षरता में भारी कमी

(D) 'सबके लिए प्रारंभिक शिक्षा' के क्षेत्र में महत्त्वपूर्ण प्रगति

Ans. (B) Higher priority given to quality and innovative initiatives in basic education

Q16. What was the vision of the National Curriculum Framework, 2005?

राष्ट्रीय पाठ्यचर्या की रूपरेखा, 2005 की कल्पना क्या थी?

Ans. Refer to Chapter-1, Q.No.-18

Q17. What is meant by 'equalisation of educational opportunity'?

'शैक्षिक अवसरों के समकरण' से क्या अभिप्राय है?

Ans. Refer to Chapter-1, Q.No.-14

Q18. State the Right to Education for the children between the age-group of 6-14 years.

6-14 वर्ष तक के सभी बच्चों के लिए शिक्षा के अधिकार का वर्णन कीजिए।

Ans. Every child of the age of 6 to 14 years shall have a right to free and compulsory education in a neighborhood school till the completion of elementary education.

Q19. Explain the role and responsibilities of the teachers to achieve the goal of cent percent literacy.

शत्-प्रतिशत साक्षरता का लक्ष्य प्राप्त करने के लिए अध्यापकों की भूमिका तथा उत्तरदायित्व को स्पष्ट कीजिए।

Ans. Refer to Chapter-1, Q.No.-26

Q20. Assess the guidance-related role of SCERT.

एस.सी.ई.आर.टी. की निर्देशन-संबंधी भूमिका का आकलन कीजिए।

Ans. Refer to Chapter-1, Q.No.-34

Q21. What type of school is a Samuh Nivasi School?

समूह निवासी विद्यालय किस प्रकार का विद्यालय है?

Ans. Refer to Chapter-2, Q.No.-7 (ii)

Q22. Calculate the Gross Enrollment Ratio (GER) if the number of children enrolled in a primary school is 40 and the number of children of primary school age is 60.

सकल पंजीयन अनुपात (GER) का प्रतिशत में अनुकूलन कीजिए यदि किसी प्राथमिक विद्यालय में पंजीकृत कुल बच्चों की संख्या 40 है तथा प्राथमिक विद्यालय आयु वर्ग के कुल बच्चों की संख्या 60 है।

Ans. The number of children enrolled in a primary school = 40
The number of children of primary school age = 60
Gross Enrollment Ration (GER) =

$$\text{Primary GER} = \frac{\text{Number of children eurolled in primary school}}{\text{Number of children of primary school age}}$$

$$= \frac{40}{60} = 0.66$$

Hence, percentage of GER = GER×100

= 0.66×100
= 66 percent (approx)

Q23. The mid-day meal programme of which State is the best in India?
भारत में किस राज्य का मध्याह्न भोजन कार्यक्रम सर्वोत्तम है?
Ans. Karnataka

Q24. What is meant by Alternative and Innovative Education (AIE)?
वैकल्पिक तथा नवाचारी शिक्षा (AIE) से क्या अभिप्राय है?
Ans. Refer to Chapter-2, Q.No.-16

Q25. How far do you agree that quality of education depends on the quality of teachers?
आप कहाँ तक सहमत हैं कि शिक्षा की गुणवत्ता अध्यापक की गुणवत्ता पर निर्भर करती है?
Ans. Refer to Chapter-2, Q.No.-16

Q26. What does planning in general denote?
सामान्य शब्दों में नियोजन किस बात का सूचक है?
Ans. Refer to Chapter-2, Q.No.-21

Q27. Explain the role of decentralisation in the field of education.
शिक्षा के क्षेत्र में विकेंद्रीकरण की भूमिका स्पष्ट कीजिए।
Ans. Refer to Chapter-2, Q.No.-19

Q28. What does quality in education include?
शिक्षा की गुणवत्ता में क्या सम्मिलित है?

Ans. Refer to Chapter-3, Q.No.-1

Q29. Why are special interventions needed for attracting and retaining tribal children in schools?

जनजातीय बच्चों को विद्यालय में आकर्षित करने के लिए तथा उन्हें वहीं विद्यालय में बने रहने के लिए विशेष तरीकों की आवश्यकता क्यों पड़ती है?

Ans. Refer to Chapter-3, Q.No.-13

Q30. Suggest any two ways to educate the children of those numerous families that rely on the income of their children.

उन अनेक परिवारों के बच्चों को शिक्षित करने के लिए कोई दो तरीके सुझाइए, जो उन बच्चों की कमाई पर निर्भर रहते हैं।

Ans. Refer to Chapter-3, Q.No.-18(i)

Q31. Mudaliar Commission recommended which two types of institutions for teacher training?

मुदालियर आयोग ने अध्यापक प्रशिक्षण के लिए किन दो प्रकार की संस्थाओं का सुझाव दिया था?

Ans. Refer to Chapter-1, Q.No.-10

Q32. Describe any two concerns of elementary education based on the recommendation of the various commissions.

विभिन्न आयोगों की सिफारिशों पर आधारित प्रारंभिक शिक्षा के किन्हीं दो सरोकारों का वर्णन कीजिए।

Ans. Refer to Chapter-1, Q.No.-16

Q33. Analyse any two areas of children's rights as categorised by a 'Canadian organisation'.

कनाडा के एक संगठन द्वारा वर्गीकृत बच्चों के अधिकारों से संबंधित किन्हीं दो क्षेत्रों का विश्लेषण कीजिए।

Ans. Refer to Chapter-1, Q.No.-30

Q34. Explain any two important functions of NCERT.

एन.सी.ई.आर.टी. के किन्हीं दो प्रमुख कार्यों की व्याख्या कीजिए।

Ans. Refer to Chapter-1, Q.No.-32

Q35. When, where and how was the National Council of Educational Research and Training established?

राष्ट्रीय शैक्षिक अनुसंधान एवं प्रशिक्षण केंद्र की स्थापना कब, कहाँ और कैसे की गई थी?

Ans. Refer to Chapter-1, Q.No.-31

Q36. List any four objectives of the Shiksha Karmi Project.

शिक्षा कर्मी परियोजना के किन्हीं चार उद्देश्यों को सूचीबद्ध कीजिए।

Ans. Refer to Chapter-2, Q.No.-5

Q37. Why are innovative activities essential to promote Sarva Shiksha Abhiyan?

सर्व शिक्षा अभियान को बढ़ावा देने के लिए नवचारी गतिविधियाँ क्यों अनिवार्य हैं?

Ans. Refer to Chapter-2, Q.No.-16

Q38. Suggest any two steps for involving community in micro-planning process.

सूक्ष्म आयोजन प्रक्रिया में समुदाय को सम्मिलित करने के लिए कोई दो चरण सुझाइए।

Ans. Refer to Chapter-2, Q.No.-22

Q39. Assess the role of the teacher educators in the development of the prospective teachers.

भावी शिक्षकों के विकास में अध्यापक शिक्षकों की भूमिका का आकलन कीजिए।

Ans. Refer to Chapter-3, Q.No.-4

Q40. Mention the four basics according to which nine articles were drafted in the conference of the World Declaration on Education.

'शिक्षा पर विश्व घोषणा' नामक सम्मेलन में किन चार आधारों पर 9 अनुच्छेदों का प्रारूप बनाया गया था? उनका उल्लेख कीजिए।

Ans. Refer to Chapter-3, Q.No.-25

Q41. Describe any five features of ancient Indian education.

प्राचीन भारतीय शिक्षा की किन्हीं पाँच विशेषताओं का वर्णन कीजिए।

Ans. Some special features of the ancient educational system as follows:

(1) The pupil was eligible to admission to the preceptor's house only on the basis of his moral fitness and unimpeachable conduct.

(2) The discipline of brahmacharya or celibacy was compulsory. Though a married youth was entitled to get education, yet he was denied the right of being the residential pupil.

(3) There was equality between the sexes in the field of knowledge.

(4) Brahman-Sangh was an organisation where meritorious students were given chances to fulfill their quest of higher knowledge.

(5) The admission was made by the formal ceremony Upanayana or initiation by which the pupil left the home of his natural parents for that of the preceptor. In this new home he had a second birth and was called Dvijya or twice born.

Q42. Identify the special problems of the deprived children of urban areas in the field of education. How can such problems be solved? Highlight the role of NGOs in this field.

शहरी सुविधावंचित बच्चों की शिक्षा के क्षेत्र में विशेष समस्याओं की पहचान कीजिए। इस प्रकार की समस्याओं को कैसे हल किया जा सकता है? इस क्षेत्र में गैर-सरकारी संगठनों की भूमिका को उजागर कीजिए।

Ans. Refer to Chapter-3, Q.No.-17

☺☺☺

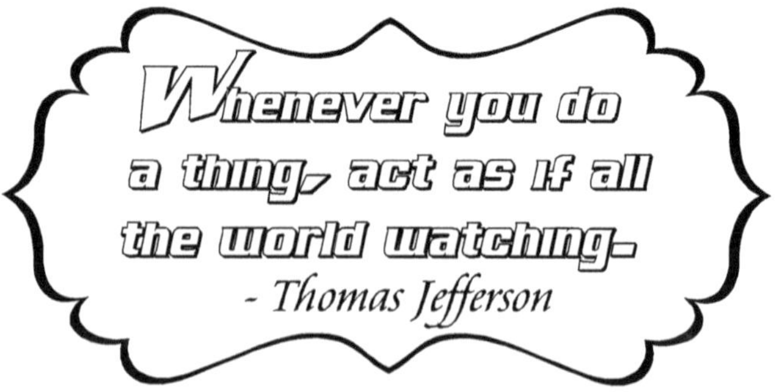

www.ingramcontent.com/pod-product-compliance
Ingram Content Group UK Ltd.
Pitfield, Milton Keynes, MK11 3LW, UK
UKHW021700190726
13853UKWH00001B/383